VIOLENCE IN OUR SCHOOLS

HALLS OF HOPE, HALLS OF FEAR

Tamra Orr

Franklin Watts
A Division of Scholastic Inc.
New York Toronto London Auckland Sydney
Mexico City New Delhi Hong Kong
Danbury, Connecticut

Photographs © 2003: AP/Wide World Photos: 160 (Barry Sweet), 96 (Mark J. Terrill), 28; Corbis Images: 46 (Rune Hellestad), 18, 34 (Reuters NewMedia Inc.); Corbis Sygma: 79; Getty Images: 139 (Tim Boyle), 134 (Chris Hondros), 39 (Newsmakers), 58; ImageState/Patrick Ramsey: 146; James Levin/Studio 10: cover; Masterfile/Pierre Tremblay: 136; Omni-Photo Communications/Jeff Greenberg: 90; Photo Researchers, NY: 158 (Richard Hutchings), 163 (Kathy Sloane); PhotoEdit/Mary Kate Denny: 144; Photri Inc.: 54, 67 (Skjold), 8; S.A.V.E.: 108; Stock Boston: 76 (Charles Kennard), 47 (Frank Siteman); The Image Works: 102 (Bob Daemmrich), 43 (Michael Siluk), 22 (Maureen Burkhart); Visuals Unlimited: 124 (Jeff Greenberg), 9, 63 (Jim Whitmer).

Book design by Joan M. Toro

Library of Congress Cataloging-in-Publication Data

Orr, Tamra.
   Violence in our schools : halls of hope, halls of fear / Tamra Orr.
      p.   cm.
   Summary: Chronicles school violence and discusses its causes, perpetrators, and solutions, including "Questions to ponder" and specific advice for individual action.
   Includes bibliographical references and index.
   ISBN 0-531-12268-9
   1. School violence—United States—Juvenile literature. [1. School violence. 2. Violence.] I. Title.

LB3013.32.O77   2003
371.7'8—dc21   2003000104

CONTENTS

WHAT IS HAPPENING?

*K*ids! *What's the matter with kids today?*
                    —*from the musical* Bye, Bye, Birdie

Adults have used that phrase for years. It seems like each new generation that comes along is just different enough from the older generation that the two can't quite understand each other. While most of the problems teens face (i.e., peer pressure, unpredictable emotions, temptations to engage in risky behavior, and so forth) have been around for decades, they change or shift in ways that make them puzzling to many grown-ups. Little throughout history has ever been as upsetting and confusing, however, as the repeated incidents of deadly school violence that have erupted in today's schools. It has everyone asking the same questions: why is this happening and what can be done about it?

The concept of school violence has been around for at least half of the century. James Dean's character was

The 1955 film *Rebel Without a Cause* focuses on an alienated and rebellious youth, who is viewed as a social outcast, searching for his identity.

the ultimate bad boy/misfit in the 1955 film *Rebel Without a Cause,* and other kids who just don't fit in and are driven by frustration and angst are constantly being featured in today's films. Many of their school years are spent trying to fit in, be popular, be academically successful, and have a good time—simultaneously. Few students ever achieve all of these goals; it's just too much to ask for most. Far too many kids are miserable and frustrated; for a select few those emotions escalate into violence. These unhappy kids are heading in a different direction; they are fighting back and doing so with firepower, sometimes even at the cost of their own lives. Where once they might have settled an argument with their fists, these kids are wielding knives and packing guns. Broken noses are being replaced by bullet holes, and what was once looked at as just typical adolescent sparring is becoming a national nightmare.

The good news in all of this is that although adolescent homicides skyrocketed in the mid-1980s, since the mid-1990s, they have fallen. Thanks to the ever-present media and some truly horrific incidents, this may not seem true, but Bureau of Justice statistics demonstrate that between 1992 and 1998, the rate of violent acts at schools went down from 48 per 1,000 children to 43 per 1,000. This means youth are making a turn for the better, which is a ray of hope in what was once a pretty dismal picture. The problem isn't gone; kids are still violent; but things can change, and you can play an active role in that change, along with your peers, your family, your school, and your community.

By playing an active role in your school and community, kids like you can make a difference in stopping school violence.

Questions to Ponder

1. What do you think are the main factors that caused the number of violent incidents to decrease in the last decade?
2. Do you think it is possible to be socially and academically successful in all ways in school? Why or why not?

The Common Myths of School Violence

Myth: The violence epidemic is over and youth are safer today than they were a decade ago.

Fact: Overall statistics on youth violence are down, but suicide is rising, as are attacks with multiple victims.

Myth: All offenders are alike, and they can be easily identified in early childhood.

Fact: Tendencies and warning signs may be present, but there is no clear-cut way to know which child will turn violent.

Myth: Child abuse will always lead to violent behavior later in life.

Fact: About one-third of the kids who are abused become violent. Experts suspect that the other two-thirds do not because they found a mentor or adult friend somewhere who helped steer them in a better direction.

Myth: Trying juveniles as adults in court will decrease the chance of teens committing more crimes.

Fact: No evidence exists as of yet that giving kids harsher sentences deters them from committing crimes. Serving out a sentence in an adult prison does make for a tough future, however, full of the potential for rape, assault, and suicide while in prison.

A Look Through History

What has been going on in the schools? What has happened that made the nation suddenly sit up and notice that something seemed to be wrong? Looking at a timeline of incidents provides quite a few clues. How many incidents of student violence have occurred since they were first recorded in 1974 is hard to determine because of the many different factors some lists include—or don't. For instance, some include suicides; others do not. Some include events involving adults or incidents that

11

occurred in college settings, while others only count those without adult involvement and only up to high school. No matter how the numbers are calculated, however, looking over the history of school violence is still a sobering experience.

The first recorded episode of violence involving a school was in Bath, Michigan, way back in May of 1927. An angry farmer named Andrew Kehoe was upset about losing his farm to foreclosure. Wanting to get revenge, he used the fact that his tax dollars were going to build a new school as his excuse for what he did next. During the preceding winter and into the spring, he brought small quantities of explosives to the school and placed all the wiring he needed to detonate them. No one thought much of his continual presence there because he worked at the school as a volunteer part-time handyman. Everything was set to go off at 9:40 A.M., just as the school day began. The explosion instantly killed thirty-eight students and two teachers and wounded more than fifty others. If the second bomb in another part of the school hadn't been spotted and defused, another 260 students and all the teachers would have died. Kehoe didn't stop there, however. While police and firefighters ran to the school, Kehoe called the school superintendent over. When the man was close enough, Kehoe fired a shotgun at his pickup truck, detonating the dynamite that was packed within it. The city's postmaster and a retired farmer who happened to be standing close by were killed in the blast. An additional victim was Kehoe's wife, whom he had killed before leaving home that morning.

The next known incident of school violence occurred more than thirty years later and was once again the result of adult anger. In September of 1959, in Houston, Texas, Paul Harold Orgeron, age forty-nine, was upset that his young son had been enrolled in a particular school. So he packed a suitcase full of dynamite and placed it in the school's playground. It exploded, killing him, his seven-year-old son, two other children, a teacher, and a school custodian. The principal and nineteen other children were injured in the blast.

Until the mid-1970s it was rare that a student was the perpetrator in an incidence of school violence. As the years progress, the incidents continue to escalate, as the timeline below shows. While more incidents have occurred than are listed here, these were some that made the biggest headlines.

Timeline of School Violence Incidents: 1974–2002

December 30, 1974
Olean, New York
Anthony Barbaro, eighteen, brought guns and homemade bombs to school and set off fire alarms. He fired at janitors and responding firefighters; he committed suicide while awaiting trial

January 29, 1979
San Carlos, California
One principal and one janitor killed; nine students and adults wounded; Brenda Spencer, sixteen, shot them with the sniper rifle she had been given for Christmas by her father

September 26, 1988	Greenwood, South Carolina One student killed, fourteen students and one teacher wounded; James William Wilson Jr., nineteen, shot elementary school students with a .22-caliber pistol
May 1, 1992	Olivehurst, California Four students killed; ten students wounded; Eric Houston, twenty, attacked them at his former high school
January 18, 1993	Grayson, Kentucky Teacher and custodian held hostage and killed by senior Gary Scott Pennington, seventeen
October 12, 1995	Blackville, South Carolina Three killed when suspended student Toby Sincino, sixteen, came to school with a .32-caliber revolver
February 2, 1996	Moses Lake, Washington Two students and one teacher killed; one student wounded when Barry Loukaitis, fourteen, opened fire on his junior high school algebra class
February 19, 1997	Bethel, Alaska Principal and one student killed; two wounded; Evan Ramsey, sixteen, used a shotgun in the high school common room
October 1, 1997	Pearl, Mississippi Two students and shooter's mother killed; seven wounded when Luke Woodham, sixteen, shot them at high school
December 1, 1997	West Paducah, Kentucky Three students killed and five wounded; Michael Carneal, fourteen, opened fire at a prayer circle in the high school hallway

March 9, 1998	Summit, Washington One student killed; two students wounded; Jeffrey Lance Pennick II, eighteen, killed them at Central Avenue Elementary School
March 24, 1998	Jonesboro, Arkansas Four students and one teacher killed; ten students wounded; Mitchell Johnson, thirteen, and Andrew Golden, eleven, shot at them from the nearby woods
May 21, 1998	Springfield, Oregon Two students and both of Kinkel's parents killed; twenty-three students wounded; Kip Kinkel, fifteen, opened fire in the high school cafeteria
June 15, 1998	Richmond, Virginia One teacher and one guidance counselor wounded; Quinshawn Booker, fourteen, shot them in the high school hallway
April 20, 1999	Littleton, Colorado Fourteen students (not including killers) and one teacher killed; twenty-three students and teachers injured; Eric Harris, eighteen, and Dylan Klebold, seventeen, shot them in the high school
May 20, 1999	Conyers, Georgia Six students wounded; Thomas Solomon, fifteen, fired a .22-caliber rifle in the high school
November 19, 1999	Deming, New Mexico One student killed; Victor Cordova, twelve, shot a .22-caliber handgun in the school's lobby

December 6, 1999   Fort Gibson, Oklahoma
                         Four students wounded; Seth Trickey,
                         thirteen, shot a 9-mm semiautomatic
                         handgun at the middle school

May 26, 2000   Lake Worth, Florida
                         One teacher killed; Nathaniel Brazill,
                         thirteen, shot him with a .25-caliber
                         semiautomatic pistol on the last day of
                         class

September 26, 2000   New Orleans, Louisiana
                         Two students ages thirteen and fifteen,
                         injured when they shot each other in a
                         fight

March 5, 2001   Santee, California
                         Two students killed; fifteen students
                         wounded; Charles Andrew Williams,
                         fifteen, shot them in the high school
                         bathroom

March 7, 2001   Williamsport, Pennsylvania
                         One student wounded; Elizabeth
                         Catherine Bush, fourteen, shot her in
                         the high school cafeteria

March 22, 2001   El Cajon, California
                         Four students and two teachers
                         wounded; Jason Hoffman, eighteen,
                         shot them in the high school

May 7, 2001   Anchorage, Alaska
                         Four students wounded; Jason Pritchard,
                         thirty-three, cut and stabbed students in
                         elementary school playground

November 12, 2001   Caro, Michigan
                         Chris Buschbacher, seventeen, took two
                         students and one teacher hostage with
                         a rifle and shotgun; all were released
                         and Buschbacher committed suicide

December 5, 2001   Springfield, Massachusetts
One principal killed; Corey Ramos, seventeen, stabbed him in a classroom

March 2, 2002   Cashmere, Washington
One student stabbed by Mike Placencia, fourteen, following a racial remark

Where will it stop—or will it? While it appears that these episodes of school shootings are overwhelming, former U.S. Secretary of Education Richard Riley stated that less than 1 percent of teenage homicides occur in schools. Many educators remind Americans that kids are far more at risk on the street, in their cars, or their homes than they are at school. "Schools are safe places to be," is what some are saying; yet the idea of kids walking into classrooms and opening fire lingers in people's minds and makes getting on the bus in the morning a lot more unnerving than it used to be. Terence Monmaney, a medical writer for the *Los Angeles Times*, phrased it this way:

> The challenge for parents, students and policymakers is deciding which version of school life is more accurate: the downward trends in violence found by the Centers for Disease Control researchers and others or the harrowing new videos of frightened students running for their lives at now infamous high schools. (Grapes 2000, 20)

Questions to Ponder

1. How did you feel when you read this list of violent events?
2. Do you feel safer at home or at school? What makes you feel that way? What would make you feel safer in both places?

A Tragedy in Colorado

It was a typical day at Littleton, Colorado's Columbine High School. Lunchtime was just around the corner, and students looking forward to some food and relaxation certainly had no idea that their lives were about to change in ways they could never have imagined.

At 11:30 A.M., two seniors, Dylan Klebold, seventeen, and Eric Harris, eighteen, came to school late—and raging. Hiding homemade pipe bombs and weapons under their now-famous long black trench

Dylan Klebold (right) and Eric Harris are captured on Columbine High School security video on the day they killed fourteen students and one teacher before killing themselves.

coats, they entered the high school at a run, yelling loudly and shooting several of the guns they had been hoarding for the past year. They hit the library the worst of all, and within a matter of minutes, fourteen students and one teacher were dead and twenty-three more were injured. As for the killers, they committed suicide, as they had planned. It was the worst school massacre in U.S. history, and one that would stun the nation.

What led these two students to attack their school? As always, hindsight is 20/20, and the signs of what was to come were blatantly obvious after the fact. However, before the shooting, clues—clear, loud clues—were given but mishandled by students, faculty, and parents alike. The police and social services knew the boys, but somehow misjudged the seriousness of their threats. Like many of the other students who have gone on rampages like this, Klebold and Harris let people know in many ways what they were planning, but they just weren't taken seriously or were completely ignored.

As the days passed and the investigation into these two boys' lives intensified, it became obvious that as horrific as this attack was, it was supposed to have been much worse. Klebold and Harris hadn't just come up with the idea of destroying their school and everyone in it on an impulse. Research found that they had actually been planning this for almost a year—and they were excellent planners. During that time they collected an arsenal of weapons—from semiautomatic guns to sawed-off shotguns—thanks to Harris's girlfriend, who helped them get the weapons from gun shows. They put together dozens of pipe bombs and then drew detailed maps and plans on just where to plant them. While several bombs were used in the attack, almost one hundred had been placed strategically in other areas. One set was supposed to have gone off miles away from the school in order to distract police. Another set had been planted in the cafeteria, and a third was put into cars in the parking lot, designed to go off after the first police officers and ambulances arrived. All of these bombs failed due to an electrical problem; if they hadn't, the death toll would have been in the hundreds, just as the two seniors had hoped.

Harris's diary confirmed their plans. He wrote of the system of silent hand signals he and Klebold had devised to send messages to each other, and they left behind a detailed videotape of their plans, stating they had a goal of killing at least 250 people. They even wondered who would play their parts once the whole event was turned into a movie. Indeed, the boys even had their own Web site on the Internet that outlined what they were planning to do and clearly announced their intentions and upcoming suicides. They sent an E-mail to the local police the night before the attack, declaring that they were simply taking revenge on all of those who had teased them and blaming teachers and parents for what was about to happen. Harris's articulate suicide note expressed the same message.

> By now, it's over. If you are reading this, my mission is complete. . . . Your children who have ridiculed me, who have chosen not to accept me, who have treated me like I am not worth their time are dead. . . . Surely you will try to blame it on the clothes I wear, the music I listen to, or the way I choose to present myself, but no. Do not hide behind my choices. You need to face the fact that this comes as a result of YOUR CHOICES. . . . You have taught these kids to not accept what is different. YOU ARE IN THE WRONG. I have taken their lives and my own—but it was your own doing. Teachers, parents, LET THIS MASSACRE BE ON YOUR SHOULDERS UNTIL THE DAY YOU DIE." (Grapes 2000, 62–63)

Therein lies the reason behind what these boys did. Overwhelmed with trying to cope in a school system and community that they felt either ignored them or despised them, they chose the only option they could think of—revenge. As big fans of violent video games, they had played innumerable games in which revenge and violence were the main modes of action, so why not?

Klebold and Harris were two examples of kids who walk the hallways of most schools today. They had long histories of being bullied, threatened, and pushed around. Most of the girls ignored them or

Columbine High School memorial site

laughed at them, while many guys did whatever they could to embarrass them and make sure they were constantly aware that they were different; they didn't belong; they were outsiders. This was one school lesson that got through loud and clear. These boys were victims, and their response to this label was to turn everyone else into victims, too.

Because of the scope of this incident, the media pounced on it. Live broadcasts hit the air, and media stations dwelled on the incident for days. In the process they tended to report some so-called facts that have since been disputed. Did the boys wear long black trench coats? Yes. Were the boys really part of a gang called the Trench Coat Mafia? Not according to a group of students who stated in an interview with the *New York Times* that that was just a small group of so-called school outcasts who hung out together, and didn't include Klebold and Harris. Were they racist and white supremacists as some news reports claimed? Not according to junior Meg Hains, one of their friends.

> I am black/white mixed. And when the media is coming up with this thing that Dylan and Eric were racist, they weren't. They were my friends. They were very nice to me, both of them. I don't get this whole racial thing that people are coming up with. (Grapes 2000, 82)

On Harris's Web site, in fact, he wrote that people who were prejudiced against any other race were wrong. "Don't let me catch you making fun of someone just because they are of a different color," he wrote (Grapes 2000, 81). Did they wear swastikas and choose Hitler's birthday for the attack as a sign of allegiance? According to classmates, this is also not true. Hains said, "They never wore swastikas around their arms. Never. Not in the entire year I've known them. No." Fellow classmate and sophomore Devon Adams said, "They're not Nazis. They didn't worship Nazis," (Grapes 2000, 82). What these two students were were lonely boys, deeply influenced by a variety of negative life experiences, who found their key to power and recognition in death, destruction, and despair.

The most chilling postscript to this massacre in Colorado is, perhaps, the copycats who came out of hiding afterward in admiration of Klebold and Harris's actions. In the weeks that followed the incident, one student threatened to finish the job, and bomb threats skyrocketed across the country. Finally, in some kind of warped praise for what these two young men did, students began wearing long black trench coats to school. A new Web site popped up on the Internet echoing the theme of "Week of the Geek," with kids cheering Klebold and Harris's decisions.

What the Statistics Have to Say

According to research from the Surgeon General, the decade from 1983 to 1993 saw an **unprecedented** rise in youth violence. Later evidence, however, has shown that since the mid-1990s, youth violence has actually been on the decline. Based on arrest records, hospital emergency room reports, and victimization data, the number of violent acts committed by young people is going down. However, other researchers state that while that may be true, suicide rates are climbing. The number of kids who admit they have committed serious, even potentially lethal, acts of physical violence has not gone down at all, and mass attacks on schools with multiple victims are increasing.

Reports are constantly being made by different organizations and groups about school violence. Here are some of the more negative figures to consider.

- One-third of U.S. students have experienced bullying, either as the target or the perpetrator, and 8 percent of those reported bullying or being bullied at least once a week (*Journal of the American Medical Association*).
- Every seven minutes a child is bullied. Four percent of the time, an adult intervenes. Eleven percent of the time, another student comes to help. Eighty-five percent of the time, there is no intervention whatsoever (Bureau of Justice).
- Forty-three percent of students fear bullying of some kind when they use the school bathroom (Bureau of Justice).
- Teachers are bullied and robbed—an average of 84 crimes per 1,000 teachers each year (Bureau of Justice).
- One in three students does not feel safe at school (Josephson Institute of Ethics).
- Almost 3 million crimes occur on or near school property every year (U.S. Department of Justice).
- Twenty percent of high school students reported they had carried a gun during the preceding thirty days (Centers for Disease Control and Prevention).
- One in five high school boys reported taking a weapon of some kind to school (Josephson Institute of Ethics).
- Seventy-five percent of boys and almost 60 percent of girls reported hitting someone in the past twelve months because they were angry (Josephson Institute of Ethics).

On the positive side of the situation, the statistics also show the following:

- Between 1993 and 1997 the number of students in grades nine through twelve who reported carrying a weapon to school during the previous thirty days declined 25 percent.
- Forty-four percent of students say that they feel more responsible for keeping their schools safe than they did in the past.
- The percentage of students who reported being victims of crime at school decreased from 10 percent to 8 percent between the years 1995 and 1999 (Bureau of Justice).
- In 1996–1997, 5,724 students were expelled for bringing a firearm to school. That figure was down to 3,523 in 1998–1999 (Bureau of Justice).

There also seems to be quite a difference between how parents and kids see the issue of school violence. According to an April 2000 *Time* magazine poll, parents were feeling better about the issue of school violence, while children were feeling worse; one-third of the surveyed children said they had personally witnessed a violent incident, while less than 10 percent of parents suspected that their children had ever seen anything.

Questions to Ponder

1. Do you think your parents look at school violence differently than you do? How so? Do you think they worry about it more or less than you do? Why?

2. Why do you think the clues that Klebold and Harris left were either ignored or mishandled? Have you ever had clues from a peer that something was wrong? How did you react to them?

GENDER EQUALITY: A FEMALE SHOOTER

One of the first school shootings to hit the press was one of the few that has had a girl at the trigger. On January 29, 1979, sixteen-year-old Brenda Spencer decided that because no one really liked the beginning of the week, she would liven things up a bit. "I just started shooting," she was reported to say. "I just did it for the fun of it. I just don't like Mondays . . . and I just did it because it's a way to cheer the day up. Nobody likes Mondays."

Armed with a .22-caliber semiautomatic gun that her father had given to her as a Christmas present, she took aim at San Diego's Grover Cleveland Elementary School from her house across the street. She waited for the principal to unlock the front doors. Once he did and the young students began to arrive, Brenda began to shoot randomly. She knew how to shoot; she had owned a BB gun for years and had practiced on windows and birds.

Spencer continued to shoot for almost twenty minutes, killing principal Burton Wragg and school caretaker Mike Suchar and injuring one police officer and nine students, ages six to twelve. Then Spencer waited for the police to arrive. For two hours she talked to the press and police negotiators before giving

Brenda Spencer's shooting spree in 1979 was one of the first school shootings committed by a female.

herself up. Spencer was sentenced to twenty-five years to life in prison on two counts of first-degree murder and assault with a deadly weapon.

In 2001 Spencer came up for parole for the second time and was once again denied. Then thirty-eight, she told the parole board at the California Institution for Women that she feels she is an entirely different person now from who she was two decades ago. "I know saying I'm sorry doesn't make it all right," she admitted in an Associated Press article. "With every school shooting, I feel I'm partially responsible. What if they got their idea from what I did?" She will be up for parole again in 2005.

According to Spencer's testimony at her parole hearing, she was taking drugs and drinking alcohol at the time of the shooting and doesn't remember much of what she said and did. Spencer also claimed for the first time that her violence was due to the fact that her father, Wallace Spencer, beat and sexually abused her. San Diego County Deputy District Attorney Richard Sachs reported that Spencer's behavior in prison had proven that she was not ready to be released.

International Violence

School shootings are not restricted to the United States, although this nation has far more of them than any other. They also seem to be caused by the same kinds of issues in other countries as they are here.

Germany has been the site of several school shootings in recent years. The biggest incident of international school violence to date occurred on April 26, 2002. A nineteen-year-old student, angry at being expelled, dressed completely in black and attacked the Gutenberg Gymnasium School in the eastern German city of Erfurt. Armed with a handgun and a pump-action weapon, he shot and killed fourteen teachers, two students, and a police officer before killing himself. Police Chief Manfred Grube described the scene as a "picture of horror." Six people were injured, and quite a few were treated for shock.

Three days later, on April 29, a seventeen-year-old student named Dragoslav Petkovic walked into his high school in the small city of Vlasenica, thirty miles northeast of Sarajevo in Bosnia and Herzegovina. He was armed with his father's 7.65-mm handgun. He shot and killed his history teacher, Stanimir Relijc, then shot and wounded math teacher Saveta Mojsilovic. Just seconds later, he killed himself. It was the country's first school shooting, and everyone was in shock. Although most people couldn't believe that Petkovic, a quiet and gentle boy, could commit such a horrific act, his classmates weren't as surprised. Continually falling grades had been very upsetting to him, and according to various newspaper reports, Ognjen Markovic, the boy's best friend, was reported to say, "He complained that the history teacher hated him and might not let him pass at the end of the year." Petkovic left a letter for his parents, thanking them for their love and support and ended it with the statement, "Forgive me. People learn from their mistakes."

A later incident in October of 2002 ended happier. A sixteen-year-old former student walked into the Friedensschule, or Peace School, in Waiblingen, Germany. He apparently entered the second-floor computer room, sat down for a little while, then stood up and pulled out a handgun. Warning all of the sixth-grade students in the room to stay calm, he called the police on a cell phone, sending the teacher and all but four students out of the room first. He demanded $1 million and a getaway car, but didn't point out any single reason for his actions. After a six-hour standoff, all of the hostages were released as the teen laid down his weapon and surrendered to the authorities.

On February 19, 2002, in Freising, Germany, an upset former student, aged twenty-two, entered his old high school and began shooting. He had just come from a factory from which he had recently been fired. There, he shot and killed his boss and injured his foreman. Next, taking a taxi, he headed for the school, where he detonated at least two homemade pipe bombs, killed the principal, wounded two teachers, and then killed himself. In January of 2000 Germany was rocked by yet another incident when a fifteen-year-old student killed his teacher in the city of Meissen. He walked into the classroom and stabbed the teacher twenty-two times. His explanation for the act was simply, "I hated her."

Sweden recently had its first incident when two teenage kids from another school killed a sixteen-year-old boy. Apparently, the boy's older brother owed these kids a little less than $485 from a drug deal. When they couldn't find the older sibling, they shot the younger one in the throat with a pistol; he died instantly. The two shooters were arrested at the scene.

Bo Munthe, the school safety professional for this school system, was quoted in Issue #25 of *Safer School News* as saying, "Most of the people on top of the pyramid believe this incident was something that will not happen again. I know it will . . . ."

In 1999 the Dutch town of Veghel, south of Amsterdam, had its first incident of school violence when a seventeen-year-old student came into the school and injured one student critically, while wounding two other students and a teacher. Rumor had it he was upset about breaking up with his girlfriend.

Japan has been the site of several incidents of youth and school violence in recent years. The most recent one was when Mamoru Takuma, the school janitor, walked into Ikeda Elementary School in Osaka and shot and killed eight children, wounding thirteen more as well as two teachers. Prior to this, a young man had dashed into another school yard and killed a seven-year-old boy with a knife.

In March of 1996, Thomas Hamilton, an adult, walked into a school in the small Highlands town of Dunblane, Scotland, and killed sixteen children and their teacher. Hamilton was one of the limited number of people permitted to own a firearm in that country.

So what is the bottom line? If overall youth violence is down, what is causing the increasing numbers of these raging attacks on schools all over the world? There are those who blame the media for it. They state that school shootings are played up so much on television and radio that it makes schools look dangerous when they still remain one of the safer places on the planet to be. Frank Zimring, a law professor at the University of California at Berkeley has been quoted as saying, "You are five times more likely to get killed on your way to school or from it than in school." Even in the face of statistics indicating declining incidents of school violence, however, it can be hard to listen to another story of another school shooting and then head off to class without a few **qualms**.

Questions to Ponder

1. Why do you think there are fewer incidents of school violence in other countries?
2. How do you weigh the differences between the positive statistics and the news reports on television?

IRONIC TIMING

About ten miles northeast of San Diego is the city of Santee, California. In 1999 when the Department of Justice gave a grant to the city's Santana High School to fund a three-year study on school violence and bullying, it had no idea of how ironic its timing would turn out to be. Midway through the study the school had an incident that would bring all their statistics and theories into the spotlight.

On the morning of March 5, 2001, fifteen-year-old Charles Andrew Williams walked into his high school armed with his dad's .22-caliber handgun.

Taking up a position in the boy's bathroom, he immediately killed Bryan Zucker, fourteen, and Randy Gordon, fifteen. He also injured eleven other students,

Driven by bullying, Charles Andrew Williams shot and killed two fellow students and wounded eleven others at Santana High School in March 2001.

a student teacher, and a school security guard before he was through. He calmly took time to reload several times, and eyewitnesses reported that he was smiling through the entire incident. After he had been captured, police found that the gun was still fully loaded with eight more rounds and ready to be fired again.

A skinny boy who had often been labeled a freak, a dork, and a nerd, Williams laid down his weapon and let the police take him into custody without a fight. In a later interview Williams's father stated that bullying had driven his son to this desperate action. Williams's public defender agreed and based his client's defense on a list of eighteen separate episodes during which others had bullied the student. These included being burned by a cigarette lighter on several occasions, being sprayed with hair spray and set on fire, and being beaten with a towel by the school pool until he was covered in welts. Classmates protested; they stated that Williams had been teased a little, but nothing serious had occurred.

Who knows what happened that pushed Williams so far over the edge that he could only perceive relief through such a violent reaction? Clues can be found in that three-year study that was going on at the time. Initial findings showed that four hundred of the school's twelve hundred students reported being the target of abusive behavior in school. Of those four hundred, half had retaliated in some way. More than one hundred and thirty students, or 11 percent, reported that they had already brought a weapon with them to school—some for protection, others to intimidate others. The final results of this study aren't known yet, but they certainly lend credence to Williams's story even as the world is appalled by his response.

WHY IS THIS HAPPENING?

Why all of these violent incidents are happening is something that everyone from distraught students and frightened parents to confused legislators and frantic administrators are asking. The answers that come back from researchers, polls, studies, and surveys range all over the place, frequently agreeing and disagreeing with each other. There appears to be no single cause of school violence, but instead a compounding of elements that combine in just the right amounts in a specific person to create a serious threat.

The causes that are brought up most frequently in discussions of school violence are

- easy access to weapons, especially guns
- prevalence of violent media (television, movies, music, videos, and computer games)
- breakdown of the family structure

- drug and/or alcohol use
- consistent bullying or teasing
- growing student involvement in gangs

While each of these separate issues seems to play a part in school violence, no single one can be blamed in and of itself. It is the combination of factors that tends to create the type of person who deals with life by picking up a weapon and creating disaster. It is easy for one group to blame another; parents can accuse schools; teachers can accuse families; everyone can accuse the media or the National Rifle Association or the drug dealers. Always pointing the finger at someone else makes the issue much easier to deal with emotionally. It puts the responsibility on someone else's shoulders—a much lighter load to bear. The fact is, however, that the blame must be placed on many contributing factors, and until that is accepted, school violence won't be effectively dealt with.

Questions to Ponder

1. Which of the factors listed above strikes you as the main cause of student violence? Why do you think it is the main one?
2. Which of the factors do you think has nothing to do with the entire issue? Why?

Gun Control

There were almost 200 million privately owned firearms in the United States as of 2000. More than 7 million are added to that figure every year. Some people strongly

Many feel that easy access to guns should be limited. This photo shows guns for sale at a Wal-Mart chain store.

believe that the sale of guns should be much more regulated so that guns stop getting into the hands of young people so easily. Experts in the area of school violence often list removing any access to guns as one of the first steps that should be taken. On the other hand, there are many people in the United States who feel that any restriction like this is in direct violation of the U.S. Constitution's Second Amendment, which they believe guarantees every person the right to bear arms. They argue that if you limit access to guns, then only the dangerous people will have them, leaving the innocent unarmed and defenseless. That debate rages on, as it has for decades.

The question does come into play, however, of what would happen if more restrictions were placed on the use of guns. Would there be an automatic drop in the frightening body count? Or would angry students, as some believe, just pick up another weapon as a replacement? Would they use knives, cars, bombs, or baseball bats? Would they still find loopholes that allow them to purchase guns or get them some other way? Well over half of the students in the United States believe they could easily obtain a gun—most often from their own homes or from friends or relatives. Arguments are often made for and against gun control laws that would limit access to weapons. While the National Rifle Association argues that limiting access to guns will only result in more crime and will leave victims with no means of self-defense, the Brady Center argues that the more guns there are, the more people will die. It often cites the example that while more than five thousand teens and children die each year of gunshot wounds in the United States, in Great Britain, where gun ownership is quite restricted, an average of fewer than twenty children die from gunshot wounds annually.

Are guns always used in a negative or destructive fashion? Are they ever helpful as protection? That is another question that surrounds the issue of whether the nation should pursue stricter gun laws. For example, in January of 2002, at Appalachian Law School in Virginia, student Peter Odighizuwa shot and killed L. Anthony Sutin, the dean of his college, as well as Professor Thomas Blackwell and student Angela Dales, but nearly all of the news reports failed to mention exactly how he was stopped. Reports mentioned that two other law students subdued the shooter; what is missing from the story is that they were able to subdue him because they each had their own guns with them. In the case of the shooting in Pearl, Mississippi, in February of 1997, what didn't make the news was the reason the vice principal was able to subdue Luke Woodham; he had his own gun with him, too.

Perhaps the solution lies in making guns safer. Some of the possibilities being considered are putting trigger locks on guns, installing electronic locks that can only be fired by people with a decoder-type ring, and reducing the number of bullets a gun can fire before it has to be reloaded. In a landmark case involving gun safety, the widow of a school violence victim went to court over the weapon that was used to kill her husband (October 2002). Pam Grunow—wife of English teacher Barry Grunow, who was killed by Nathaniel Brazill in 2000—believes the Raven .25-caliber handgun (often referred to as the Saturday night special) used was unusually dangerous and lacked the safety devices, such as a gun lock, that could have prevented a minor from firing it. On January 27, 2003 the jury ordered gun distributor Valor Corporation to pay Pam Grunow $1.2 million in damages. Through this case, which was heard in West Palm Beach, Florida, she hopes to get cheap guns off the streets and out of the hands of children.

Questions to Ponder

1. Do you think gun control is a good or bad idea? How do you think it would affect crime overall and, in particular, incidents of school violence?
2. Do you think gun manufacturers have a responsibility to make their guns affordable or to make them safe? How can they do both?

Media Violence

Many different fingers point at the United States's fascination with violent entertainment as the primary cause of youth violence. Violence is considered to be a learned behavior, and quite a few experts believe that in this society, violence is a form of entertainment that teaches students of all ages some horrible lessons. Studies have shown that kids who do not spend a lot of time watching videos, playing video and computer games, or visiting chat rooms and Web sites on the Internet have better grades, fewer feelings of alienation, and more positive feelings about the quality of life. Other experts disagree, however; they feel that experiencing media violence of any kind will not affect a mentally healthy and happy kid. It is the child on the edge whose actions will be influenced by the experience.

The media culprits are usually divided into three catagories: television and movies, music, and video games/computer games.

Television and Movies

Violence of all kinds can be found on television, from Saturday-morning cartoons to prime-time cop shows. Statistics abound on how many thousands of acts of violence the average child will see by the time he or she turns eighteen; the usual reference is 16,000 simulated murders and 200,000 separate acts of other types of violence, most of which go completely unpunished. Action movies carry fifty to three hundred acts of violence jam-packed into two hours or less. Violence is usually glamorized and sanitized; there is often little connection shown between actions and actual pain or injury. Kids love to watch these shows and films, but what effect is it actually having on them? Many experts believe that seeing repeated acts of violence like this

Violence is a common theme in many films and television programs. These fifteen-year-olds are watching the violent movie *Natural Born Killers.*

makes a child become hardened against it—dehumanized or **desensitized** to the pain he or she is viewing.

The majority of these shows tends to perpetuate the false ideas that most people are virtually damage-proof or even immortal. Actors jump from tall buildings, get hit by trucks, or duel vicious opponents, and instead of suffering anything from broken bones to death, they just get up and keep on going. If they do happen to die, it's no big deal, since they will pop up again in the next movie, show, or commercial. This makes violence look okay—and not really very dangerous, especially if you are the "good guy." The so-called good guy commits almost half of the violent acts in a movie anyway, and he or she is often portrayed as settling problems mainly through violence. Mediation and discussion just do not play a part in movie scripts. Researchers worry that troubled kids will look at these films and see them not just as imaginative stories, but as actual game plans for their future.

Music

Is rock music truly a menace? That question was first asked in the 1950s, when an effort to ban rock music from the radio was a high priority. However, it didn't work then and it isn't likely to work now. Jann S. Wenner, editor and publisher of *Rolling Stone*, writes, "We're going to let rock and roll off the hook this time . . . rock is too popular to blame" (Grapes 2000, 69). With little doubt, music is important to most kids, and it can influence them. Most teachers know that one of the best ways to make material easier to learn is to put it to music. Socrates spoke about music and stated that he thought it was one of the strongest instruments because the rhythm and harmony can find their way deep inside a person and hold on. Former Secretary of Education William Bennett agrees heartily and adds, "Rhythm and harmony are still fastening themselves onto children's souls; today, however, much of the music they listen to is imparting mournfulness, darkness, despair, a sense of death" (Grapes 2000, 59). The repetition of words put to notes and a regular beat usually will make them easier to learn and remember. The music can often make listeners feel emotions, frequently negative emotions, that are within the lyrics.

The concern over music was intensified when the fact hit the press that Eric Harris and Dylan Klebold were singer Marilyn Manson fans. Manson's lyrics tend to be rather graphic and often violent in nature. According to reports, the boys particularly liked Manson's "Irresponsible Hate Anthem," which contains the lyrics

Hey victim, should I black your eyes again?
Hey victim/You were the one who put the stick in
    my hands
I am the ism, my hate's a prism
Let's just kill everyone and let your God sort
    them out.

Did listening to lyrics like these inspire the boys to take up weapons, or did it just bolster the thoughts that were already brewing? Were the lyrics evil or just typical of what teens tend to listen to at this age? In an article

Lyrics written by Marilyn Manson have come under attack for being the cause of bad behavior in teens.

called "The Devil in Your Family Room," Salon.com writer Fiona Morgan reflects back on her own teenage years and the music she listened to. Like many other teenagers, she experienced feelings of loneliness, anger, and fear, and she believes the expression of these emotions in popular song lyrics are what attracts teens to that music in the first place. It validates their feelings and makes them feel less isolated.

Video Games/Computer Games

The majority of video games kids play are based on some form of violence. They are complex, interactive, and obviously highly entertaining. Research shows that many of the actions used in these games are based on the same training tactics the military uses, and that is quite a concern to some. Games are usually backed with repetitive music also, making the tricks and steps easier to remember later. The goal is to kill/win and often involves weaponry and a high level of violence.

The Americans for Gun Safety Foundation argues that the use of guns in video games portray guns "in an irresponsible manner and without any consequences" to their use.

In turn, kids who spend lots of time on the Internet are also a cause for alarm to some researchers. If they are there to study or find information for school, that is one thing; however, the majority are either playing violent games on Web sites or with game discs or spending time in chat rooms that may be potentially dangerous. Some families install filters on their computers so only certain sites can be accessed.

Dr. Dewey Cornell of the University of Virginia testified on "The Psychology of the School Shootings" at the House Judiciary Committee Oversight Hearing to Examine Youth Culture and Violence in May of 1999. He is a firm believer that the violence in media is what gives troubled kids the motivation to do what they do. "To charge into a building and try to kill as many people as possible is an enactment of video violence," he said. "This is the kind of violence you see in movies and play on video games. Children of today live in a social environment where violence is a primary form of entertainment, and they are exposed to values and ideas that reinforce and glorify violence." Cornell goes on to say that adults are more protected from false advertising by salespeople than today's youth are from "these salesmen of hate and violence." "As a society," he adds, "we must be more concerned about the daily doses of extreme violence administered to our children through television, video games, music, and the Internet." He believes that seeing messages of violence and hatred over and over makes youth numb to it, interferes with their own idea of personal safety, and confuses their own feeling about harming others.

On the opposite side of the argument are those who believe violent video games may just serve as a stress outlet for many kids. In a *New York Times* interview with eight Columbine high school students just after the shooting, seventeen-year-old junior Meg Hains said,

> I have played the game Doom that they're saying Dylan and Eric constantly played. And I don't think it was that game. I'd go to school, and there were people that would so royally p—s me off and I'd just go home and I'd sit on that game for hours, just taking out my stress on it. And the next day, I'd be perfectly fine. That's the way I get rid of my stress, instead of going out and really killing people. . . . I know this sounds weird, but some violent games are a therapy for kids." (Grapes 2000, 89–90)

Questions to Ponder

1. Do you think the media is a valid issue when it comes to school violence? Which one seems to have the most influence on you personally: television, music, or video games? Why?
2. Do you think that media should be censored, that is, should song lyrics, game scenes, and television programming be limited as to what they can and cannot include?

The Influence of Family

In a national Gallup poll taken in April of 2001, people of all ages were asked what they thought was the single most important thing that could be done to prevent another school shooting. Their number-one choice (31 percent) was increased parental involvement and responsibility. Fourteen percent voted for more security in schools, and 11 percent voted for better gun control laws. When asked what they thought was the number-one cause of school violence, they again chose parenting and home life first. Availability of guns and violence in the media ranked second and third. The conclusion of the Gallup poll was that most people feel that the impact of parents and the family play the main role in preventing school shootings. Adults seem to feel that the chances of such incidents continuing to happen are high until some immediate improvements are made in family life and parenting.

Parents obviously have an incredible influence on children, but should they have to shoulder all of the blame for everything if something goes drastically wrong? The family structure has gone through a lot of changes in the last few decades, and some of the changes have not had positive effects. In many homes both parents are working and inaccessible many hours of the day or evening, and this has not been a positive development for many kids who need some extra one-on-one time with their moms or dads or really could use some additional supervision. Many parents struggle with appropriate discipline—too much or too little can have an impact. Divorce is a common factor for many families also, and it isn't unusual for kids never to see one of their parents on any kind of regular basis, if at all. Other families deal with issues such as neglect and abuse, both of which greatly increase the risk of a child growing up violent. Kids who are abused or who are witnesses to abuse have a far greater chance of becoming abusers themselves than those who never experienced that kind of trauma.

Questions to Ponder

1. What do you think the role of the family is in school violence?
2. What changes do you think the average family (or your own) needs to make to improve the situation?

Drug and Alcohol Use

While initial findings show that drug use in youth has decreased slightly, alcohol use remains fairly steady. The regular use of either can only affect a student adversely. Of course, there is also a new slant to the factor of drug use: the prescription medication some kids are already on. Some researchers believe there is a connection between the violent acts some kids commit and the prescription drugs they are taking. Shawn Cooper was on Ritalin when he attacked; Kip Kinkel had been taking Ritalin and Prozac, T.J. Solomon, from Georgia, was on Ritalin when he shot his classmates, and Eric Harris was on Luvox (an antidepressant that is a cousin to Prozac). Ritalin is a medication that is often given when a student is diagnosed with attention deficit disorder (ADD) or attention deficit hyperactivity disorder (ADHD).

According to Dr. Peter Breggin, author of *Talking Back to Ritalin* and *Talking Back to Prozac*, Luvox has been strongly linked with side effects of anger, hostility, and the desire to attack or take revenge. In a study by Yale researchers published in the March 1991 *Journal of the American Academy of Child and Adolescent Psychology*, scientists studied the effect of Prozac on adolescents. According to the study, at least one twelve-year-old taking Prozac began having nightmares about killing his classmates at school. When he was taken off the medication, the nightmares stopped. When he was again put on Prozac, they returned.

In an essay titled "Children and Psychiatric Drugs," John Breeding, Ph.D., writes that a great deal of research has shown that agitation and violence are well-known side effects of certain drugs, including Ritalin and Prozac. Kelly Patricia O'Meara, a reporter for *Insight on the News,* wrote an essay called "The Link Between Psychiatric Drugs and School Shootings." In it, she states that there is quite a bit of evidence that Ritalin and other related stimulants can produce symptoms such as the inability to sleep, imagining things, acting on impulse, and hyperactivity. "And," she writes, "the DEA's [Drug Enforcement Administration] list of potentially adverse effects of Ritalin includes **psychosis**, depression, dizziness, insomnia, nervousness, irritability, and attacks of Tourette's or other tic syndromes" (Grapes 2000, 55).

Whether medications such as Ritalin and Prozac play a role in youth violence is still unknown. Many physicians and researchers believe there is a link, but there are many who do not. The possibility exists, however, and should not be completely dismissed.

Questions to Ponder

1. What role do you think alcohol and recreational drugs play in school violence?
2. Do you think prescription medications such as Ritalin or Prozac are a factor in how some students react to life? Why or why not?

Bullying and Teasing

In a variety of surveys conducted with school students, when asked why they think their fellow classmates have resorted to killing people, the vast majority (almost 90 percent) stated that it was most likely to get back at those people who hurt, teased, or bullied them. According to a survey by the Josephson Institute of Ethics (1998 and 2000), 43 percent of high school boys thought it was okay to hit or threaten a person who made them angry. Revenge seems to be the motivation for almost every single school shooting of the last decade. Children are committing violence to release or express their feelings of rage and rejection; it is their opportunity to achieve a real role reversal, and just for once have control over those who they feel have controlled them for so long.

This idea of revenge, or **retaliation,** is a prevalent one in all of the research on school shootings. Kids who already have several counts against them— for example, a low-income family coupled with abusive parents—can find themselves being labeled as "nerds," "wimps," "homos," "fags," "geeks," "losers"; the

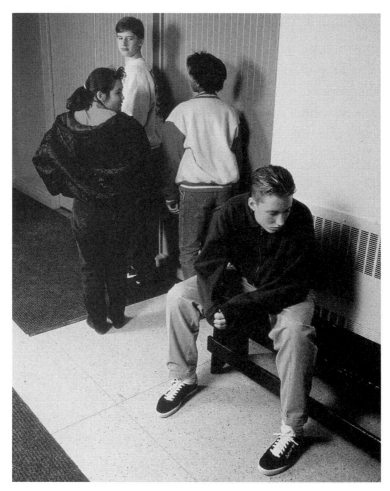

One of the most common reasons for school violence is retaliation from being bullied and teased.

kids who everyone knows are easy to pick on in school. Go ahead and call them names, attack them, steal from them—it's okay because they won't fight back. For many, that treatment is the last straw; it's what takes the quiet kid who won't fight back and turns him or her into a force that brings **irrevocable** destruction.

A look inside the journals of several high school shooters provides insight into what they were thinking. In Kip Kinkel's journal he wrote, "Hate drives me. . . . I am so full of rage. . . . Everyone is against me. . . . As soon as my hope is gone, people die." He felt this way despite the fact that he came from a financially secure and well-educated family and had already been in therapy. Luke Woodham wrote in his journal,

> I am not insane. I am angry. I am not spoiled or lazy, for murder is not weak and slow-witted. Murder is gutsy and daring. . . . I killed people because people like me are mistreated every day. . . . I am malicious because I am miserable. (*Chicago Sun Times,* October 15, 2000)

TALKING IT OUT: FINDING A CONFIDANTE

One of the keys to coping with all the emotions and pressures of adolescence is finding someone to trust and confide in. Many experts believe that if some of the teens in prison today for violent offenses had had someone to talk to about their anger, confusion, and loneliness, they would not have committed crimes.

Teens need someone they can trust, someone who will listen and understand. It must be someone who believes and supports them and can help guide them to a better understanding of themselves and the world

---

around them. Research has shown, for instance, that teens who spend time talking to their parents have a much lower risk of using drugs or violence to help them to cope with life. They often have more confidence and high self-esteem also—all **deterrents** to acts of violence.

While parents can be the best people to have as confidants because they usually know their children well and care about them more than anyone else would, it doesn't always work out that way. Other choices are

- teachers
- relatives
- neighbors
- ministers/clergy
- coworkers
- counselors
- friends
- hot lines
- organizations (YMCA, youth groups, and so forth)

Confiding feelings and thoughts in someone who truly cares is often the quickest, best way to defuse strong emotions that otherwise might lead to heartbreak and worse.

Doing Time: Prison Sentences for School Violence

There should be some standard that determines how children are sentenced when they commit a violent crime in school, but it is apparently rather hard to find. Many times the punishment is based on the climate of society at that moment; if people are focused on the issue of school violence, sentences might be tougher than if their attention is focused elsewhere. Sentences can also vary depending on whether the child had any prior history of crime or arrests, what the intent of the action was, if the incident took preplanning or if it was a spur-of-the-moment attack, and if the child was a leader, single perpetrator, or following someone else's lead. "There is an incredible amount of leeway in sentencing," says Phil Burns, author of *Multiple Victims, Multiple Causes*. "It ranges from the ridiculous—like only going to jail on the weekends so you can stay in school, to the absurd—like three hundred plus years." "Let's face it," he adds, "if prisons worked, we would be tearing them down, not building more. Rehab isn't working, and you can't turn a kid around without counseling."

Laws against these juvenile offenders have changed quite a bit in the last decade. In 1994 President Clinton's Violent Crime Control and Law Enforcement Act federalized many of the states' changes, authorizing adult prosecution of kids thirteen and older who are charged with certain offenses and expanding the death penalty to cover sixty different crimes. By 2000, forty-five states had adopted new laws or altered old ones to make it easier to prosecute these young perpetrators. California Proposition 21, for instance, once called the Gang Violence and Juvenile Crime Prevention Act, extended the jurisdiction of criminal courts to include prosecution of teen offenders fourteen years and older as adults rather

Teenage inmates inside lockdown at a jail complex for juveniles in Phoenix, Arizona.

than as minors. In 2000 the new law passed 62.1 percent to 37.9 percent. It also set up new regulations regarding juvenile records; they are often no longer sealed, and are open and available for others to read.

The attitude toward juvenile offenders now is if they can do the crime, they can do the time. If these teens are processed as adults, they usually receive adult sentences, which are to be served in adult prisons. About one in ten convicted juveniles is serving his or her time in an adult prison. Some believe that severely prosecuting these kids will act as a deterrent to committing crimes in the first place. Others believe, however, that sending them to prison will only result in more tragedies. "There's a new attitude of getting tough with teens," says Professor Leo Sandy. "This is unbelievably stupid thinking. Take a kid in a rage, punish him with prison time, and he comes out a still raging, hardened criminal with skills." For many of these teens, suicide, rape, and assault are a daily threat. Andrew Vachss, attorney for matters concerning children and youth and well-known author of such books as *The Life-Style Violent Juvenile: The Secure Treatment Approach*, wrote in his article "Little Adult Criminals" in the May 23, 2001, issue of the *New York Times*,

> A civilized society must not easily give up hope of rehabilitating a child who commits a crime. While a 17-year-old repeat offender may warrant trial as an adult criminal, children who are 12 or 14 do not possess the emotional maturity to control their impulses or to fully understand the consequences of their actions. It is more than social development; recent medical research has found that the brain continues to develop into one's teenage years. In no instance does a juvenile belong in adult prisons.

In an article titled "Young Voices from the Cell" in *Time* magazine (May 20, 2001), two journalists interviewed twelve young convicted school shooters. It was a sobering experience. The boys' sentences varied greatly—from less than ten years to well over a hundred. Mitchell Johnson and Andrew Golden from Arkansas are expected to be released before they hit twenty-one. Evan Ramsey from Alaska had been sentenced to more than two hundred years, and during the short time he has been in his maximum-security prison, he has already been in solitary confinement following an incident of beating.

Andrew Wurst has already attempted suicide. Kentucky's Michael Corneal is in for life, and Kip Kinkel from Oregon received 112 years despite an appeal in October of 2002. "Almost all the shooters were expressing rage, either against a particular person for a particular affront or, more often, against a whole cohort of bullying classmates," write Timothy Roche and Amanda Bower about the prisoners. The majority of them have also been diagnosed with some kind of mental illness—including depression, personality disorders, or **schizophrenia**—since their incarceration, and half had been, or are, on Ritalin.

Charles "Andy" Williams had faced a possible prison sentence of up to 435 years for his shootings at Santana High School; however, on August 15, 2002, a San Diego judge changed it to fifty years to life, the minimum possible term. Judge Herbert Exarhos stated that a longer term would have meant, in all reality, life imprisonment, and he did not feel he could do that. According to both the judge and Williams's parents, Williams is quite remorseful and has continuing nightmares about what happened. He will be at least sixty-five when he is released—a lifetime for him and not nearly long enough for some of his victims. Deputy District Attorney Kristin Anton was quoted as saying, "His freedom should be taken away forever." His father, Jeff, stated on ABC News's *Good Morning America* that he hoped his son would someday get the chance to do something good with his life. "I hope the judge will find a sentence somewhere in between so Andy will have a chance to get out of prison sixty, seventy years down the road from now." During the sentencing, Williams's feelings were evident. "I feel horrible about . . ." he began, but his voice trailed off into sobs, and he quietly added that he wished he had never gotten out of bed that day. "It really hurts me . . . I'm responsible for . . . for all this stuff," he added.

Questions to Ponder

1. Do you have a confidant? Someone who you can trust and talk to about anything? If not, who could you choose? If so, how does talking to him or her make things better?
2. What do you think about the sentencing that violent youths get? Is it fair or unfair? How would you change it to make it most appropriate?

CHAPTER THREE

WHO IS DOING IT?

The question of just who is attacking today's schools in unprecedented numbers is an extremely complicated one. While there certainly is a profile of what kind of kid tends to commit these crimes, it is also a dangerous notion that this is the only kind of kid who does. Some argue, in fact, that there is no solid or reliable profile of a school shooter. As law enforcement, justice systems, and school systems start to profile students or put together a picture of what the typical school shooter is like, they run the very high risk of stereotyping kids. There is great concern among many researchers that by pointing at any one set of characteristics, kids will get labeled, judged, and tried before they ever do anything wrong. For example, just because Klebold and Harris happened to wear long trench coats when they went on their killing spree, does this mean that any student wearing a trench coat is suspect? Should trench coats be banned from school just for this reason? If a person is listening to Marilyn Manson songs or playing a game of Doom, should he or she be put on a suspect list? It is a real balancing act to have a heightened awareness of what to look for based on previous evidence and still not overreact to students' behaviors,

Though a profile is in place that offers a picture of what type of kid commits violent acts, profiling can lead to stereotyping.

thereby **stigmatizing**, humiliating, or isolating them even further with erroneous labels. "Moreover," states a Secret Service researcher in a 2000 report, "the use of profiles carries a risk of overidentification. The vast majority of students who fit any given profile will not actually pose a risk of targeted violence."

Tips for Staying Safe at School

- Don't join any kind of gang.
- Report any threat of violence or weapon you know about, whether it's just a rumor or firsthand evidence.
- Don't ignore your concerns about students who talk about aggression and revenge. Help them connect with an adult to find help and support.
- Tell someone you trust of any worries or concerns you might have.
- Don't go alone to any places in the school where violence is more likely to occur (e.g., dark corners, locker rooms, rest rooms, empty classrooms, and so forth).
- Don't ever use a weapon of any kind to protect or defend yourself.
- Don't be alone during school transition times, such as right before or after school starts.
- Get involved with some kind of antiviolence group or start a chapter in your school.

The Typical Picture

Psychologists and other experts are working to paint a clear picture of the type of kid who is apt to go out and commit some kind of violent crime. As mentioned above, such a profile can be misleading and dangerous. There are certainly common denominators that can be considered, but they are not proof positive of anything. A look at many of the perpetrators shows that some elements are common: the shooter is virtually always a healthy Caucasian male of above-average intelligence, average age fifteen years, from a middle to low socioeconomic class. That doesn't always hold true. There have been African American, Hispanic, and female school shooters, there have been kids under thirteen and over eighteen, and there have been perpetrators from all social classes. The majority (again, not all) have been bullied, threatened, harassed, and teased about their height, weight, style of dress, sexual preference (real or imagined), or just their personalities in general. These are the class geeks, nerds, losers, fags, queers—these are the different ones who don't fit in with any of the set cliques. They aren't popular, athletic, rich, or brilliant. Instead, they are relative loners with only a few friends—other geeks, often bored with life and possessing an overall "life sucks" attitude. These are angry kids who sit silently in the classroom, usually causing little to no trouble; who don't seem to respond much at all to the slurs targeted at them; who seem completely disconnected from the world around them.

If a person could take a peek inside these kids' home lives, he or she would commonly see a long history of abuse and neglect, although not always. They have been harshly and/or inconsistently disciplined; they threw temper tantrums from a young age; they fight with their siblings and seem suspicious of the world around them. It isn't unusual to discover that their parents have struggled with drugs and/or alcohol abuse or that one or both have been in prison. Evan Ramsey's parents, for instance, followed that pattern. His father had been in prison, and his mother was an alcoholic. Kids with violent tendencies also tend to come from families where they witnessed repeated cases of domestic violence or child abuse. While this may not be true for every shooter's family—Klebold's and Harris's families, for example— it fits the majority. Their episodes of serious violence are often just a continuation of a life that was already filled with struggle, unhappiness, and lack of close ties to anyone.

A potential shooter is both desperately lonely at times and very self-centered. The teenage years are often a time when teens are focused on their own needs and wants over anyone else's, but these kids go even further. They believe, many times, that the actions of people around them reflect directly on them. In other words, if two kids are whispering in the back of the room or laughing over to the side, these potential shooters are most likely going to feel the kids are whispering about and/or laughing at them. They feel life treats them unfairly—which, in several ways, it does— and become quite self-absorbed. Everything is about

School shooters often feel a sense of loneliness, disconnection, and sadness.

THEM, and they have little or no concern for others. They commonly **vacillate** between feelings of complete worthlessness and total superiority. What is amazing is that despite of all that is going on under the surface of these students' lives, on the outside they are usually considered decent to good students who rarely cause any trouble in the classroom. However, as their needs fail to be met anywhere—neither at home nor at school—anger and complete frustration begin to build. Instead of dropping out and leaving school, some of these students become depressed and suicidal and others decide to commit the one act that they somehow feel will help them to connect with it.

Questions to Ponder

1. Do you think creating a common profile of a school shooter is a good idea or a bad one? Why? How can it help and/or harm?
2. Do you recognize the description of the students presented in this chapter? How does it change your perspective on other students in your class?

Shootings and Gender Studies

It is little surprise to most psychologists that virtually every school shooter is male. Adolescent boys have up to eighteen times the amount of **testosterone** in their systems as they had just a few years earlier, and this hormone has a direct link to aggressive behavior. According to the U.S. Department of Justice, males commit violent acts six times more often than females do—and far more serious crimes at that. This means that there is one violent male offender for every nine males ten years old and up, while there is only one violent female offender for every fifty-six females ten years old and up. William Pollack, psychologist, consultant to the Secret Service, and author of *Real Boys: Rescuing Our Sons from the Myths of Boyhood,* writes about the "boy code," an unwritten set of rules that guide male behavior. It is comprised of four guidelines: the "sturdy oak" attitude—boys should never show any form of weakness; the "give 'em hell" attitude—boys should have a macho image and act tough and rough; the "big wheel" attitude—boys should achieve status, power, and dominance; and the "no-sissy-stuff" attitude—real boys should never express any emotion except anger (Aronson 2000, 97–98). However, following the code doesn't really solve anything. Many of these school shooters took the teasing and taunting "like a man." They stayed cool on the outside and never let anyone see them sweat—or cry. They certainly followed through on the macho rule, too, because what can be more manly than mowing down your enemies with fire-power, shouting and yelling as you go? Pollack is also quoted in an article in the *Chicago Sun-Times* as saying,

> I believe they [school shooters] are all boys because the way we bring up boys in America predisposes them to a sense of loneliness and disconnection and sadness. When they have additional pain, additional grievances, they are less likely to reach out and talk to someone, less likely to be listened to. Violence is the only way they start to feel they can get a result.

In an article entitled "The Classroom Avenger" in *The Forensic Examiner* (May/June 1999), authors James P.

McGee, Ph.D. and Caren DeBernardo, Psy.D. put together a long list of qualities, or traits, that are NOT usually seen in school shooters. This is an entirely different perspective, and the list includes the following:

- Female
- Resident of a large city
- Member of a minority
- Openly homosexual/bisexual
- Member of a mainstream religious group
- Member of student government; participate in Boy/Girl Scouts, theater, choir, dance, or team sports
- Private-school student
- Outgoing, friendly, humorous
- Popular among peers
- Recipient of awards or scholarships
- Volunteer
- Pacifist
- No guns in home
- Body piercing/tattoos
- Physical handicap
- Mental retardation
- Chronic truancy
- Supportive of gun control
- Severe learning disability

Snapping or Strategy?

Some of the young men who have walked into their schools and opened fire have been called rampage killers by the media. However, this is a **misnomer**. These boys did not usually act on impulse; they didn't just snap from the weight of their lives and run home for a loaded gun. Instead, many of these boys planned everything out. They drew maps, made lists, and developed detailed strategies for what they were going to do. Often they would enlist the help of friends or girlfriends; for several, the support of their peers is what made them go through with their attacks.

When these students came into their schools loaded down with weapons and hatred, it was the ultimate role reversal. The nerds who always let others push them around and control their lives were the ones in power now. Holding a weapon—especially a gun, a weapon of real power—made them feel strong, invincible, and even happy. Klebold and Harris were reported to have shouted and laughed after each shot; Barry Loukaitis stood over a dying student and said, "Sure beats algebra, doesn't it?" Even Brenda Spencer, one of the few female shooters, smiled as she was led away by the police and muttered that she had killed people because "everyone hated Mondays anyway." These kids are lashing out; they are exploding and letting all that emotion and frustration with their world and their places in it out at once. It isn't a sudden snapping, but a slow accumulation of hurt, anger, and loneliness that builds over time. They are finally at the point where they want the rest of the world to know just how angry they are.

For anyone to think that these miserable teens are just "going through a phase" or will simply "grow out of it" is a huge, and occasionally deadly, mistake. They need help as early as possible. Shawn A. Johnston, a San Francisco forensic psychologist, suggests that by third grade it is possible to identify kids who are at risk of engaging in some form of aggression. By fifth grade, he says, experts can make relatively accurate predictions of future arrests just by looking at the number of discipline problems the child has had during the school year and the amount of negative behavior with classmates on the playground.

Top Ten Warning Signs of a Student in Serious Trouble
(according to the American Psychological Association)

1. Daily loss of temper
2. Vandalism and/or property damage
3. Announced threats to hurt self or others
4. Increase in risk-taking behaviors
5. Carrying a weapon
6. Frequent physical fighting
7. Stated, detailed plans for violence
8. Hurting animals
9. Gang membership
10. Drug and/or alcohol abuse

The U.S. Department of Education's report "Early Warning, Timely Response" lists the following warning signs as an aid to identifying and referring children who may need help:

- Social withdrawal
- Excessive feelings of isolation
- Excessive feelings of rejection
- Being the victim of violence
- Feelings of being picked on or persecuted
- Little interest in school and poor academic performance
- Expression of violence in writings and drawings
- Uncontrolled anger
- Pattern of impulsive or chronic hitting and other bullying behaviors
- History of discipline problems
- Past history of violent or aggressive behavior
- Intolerance for differences
- Drug and/or alcohol use
- Affiliation with gangs
- Access to, possession of, or use of firearms
- Serious threats of violence

Self-Violence: The Threat of Suicide

Chris Joyner was a seventh-grader at North Carolina's Zebulon Middle School, and although he was picked on now and then, it was just the usual rite of passage that many young schoolboys must go through—or so it seemed. However, on March 24, 2000, Chris excused himself from gym class to go to the rest room, and while he was there, he tied a rope around his neck and hanged himself.

Fifteen-year-old Hannah Taylerson was distraught over problems she was having with her boyfriend. She was upset about the gossip going around school about her, and in the past she had been known to cut herself when stressed. To show the world how miserable she was this time, she went home from school and hanged herself in her bedroom closet.

In Japan a thirteen-year-old boy hanged himself in a railway rest room, leaving a note that two classmates had bullied him to the point at which he no longer wanted to live. His parents then filed a 22-million yen lawsuit against the Tokyo government and the parents of the two alleged bullies, declaring that their son's death was due to *ijimi*, or bullying.

As serious as homicides may be in school, suicides are often an even bigger problem. According to the Centers for Disease Control and Prevention, at least 15 percent of all violent deaths in U.S. schools are suicides. Each year, thousands of young people between the ages of fifteen and twenty-four kill themselves. Several hundred between ten and fourteen do also. The Surgeon General states that a youth commits suicide every two hours in the United States. The rate of suicide for this age group has tripled since 1960, and suicide is one of the leading causes of death in adolescents and among college youth.

While suicide has certainly been closely linked with depression, it is rare for depression to be the sole cause. Instead, it is usually depression coupled with recent or ongoing stressful events, such as a romantic breakup, failure in school, a fight with a friend, physical or sexual abuse, or a family problem.

More than four times as many males as females die by suicide. However, females attempt suicide three times more often than males do. Attempted suicides outnumber successful ones by about eight to one; in other words, for every eight suicide attempts, one will succeed. More than half of these acts of self-violence are committed with some kind of firearm.

These are the primary warning signs and/or risk factors for people who might be prone to suicide. Note how similar they are to the warning signs of violence.

- Previous suicide attempts
- Family history of suicide
- Significant alcohol or drug use
- Having a firearm in the house
- Threatening/communicating thoughts of suicide, death, dying, or the afterlife
- Sudden increase in moodiness, withdrawal, or isolation
- Major change in eating/sleeping habits
- Feelings of hopelessness, guilt, or worthlessness
- Poor control over behavior
- Drop in quality of school performance/interest
- Lack of interest in usual activities
- Getting in trouble with authority figures
- Perfectionism
- Depression
- Personal experience of some kind of violence
- Giving away important possessions
- Hinting at not being around in the future/saying good-bye

It's important to remember that warning signs of suicide can be verbally direct statements ("I don't want to live anymore") to verbally indirect ("Soon this will all be over"). They may also be behavioral (tears, silence, insomnia) or environmental (family violence, sexual abuse, problems at school). Sexual identity issues can also lead a youth to suicide. Having any kind of firearm in the house is a serious risk; statistics show that the risk of a successful suicide is five times greater if there is a gun already in the home.

Occasionally, unhappiness and anxiety in a child will lead to the planning of his or her own suicide by killing as many other people as he or she can before dying. A number of school shooters had this attitude; Klebold and Harris killed themselves, and Ramsey intended to but couldn't follow through with it in the end.

If a kid feels suicidal, help must be found immediately. Calling 1-800-SUICIDE is a possibility; local crisis

Mental health workers answer calls at a suicide hot line crisis center.

centers are also commonly available. Talking to someone trustworthy can always help. Writing down thoughts in a journal or diary is frequently a positive way to let out emotions that are hard to share. If someone states that he or she is feeling suicidal, he or she should be taken seriously. Ways to help this person include connecting him or her with a suicide prevention program and listening carefully to how he or she feels and expressing care and empathy.

Questions to Ponder

1. How could you help someone who you suspected was suicidal?
2. What reactions and feelings did you have as you read over the Top Ten Warning Signs of a Student in Serious Trouble?

Who Are the Victims?

Every day, students and teachers are attacked on school grounds. Some people seem to be particularly vulnerable to attack, including the following:

- Younger students
- Minority students
- New students
- Possible/actual homosexual students
- Strict teachers
- Male students
- Urban school students (nine times more likely to be shot than those in rural schools)

Looking around the standard classroom and being able to point out who is apt to come to school tomorrow with a loaded gun just isn't possible. However, looking around and pointing out the person who is teased most often or who has been bullied in the gym locker room, who seems totally detached from his or her surroundings, is not so difficult. It is these invisible students who easily may be walking around like volcanos that are just waiting for the right moment to erupt. How many of them might be deterred by just a simple act of kindness or interest? The tragic answer is that no one will ever know because more times than not, it just doesn't happen.

UP CLOSE AND PERSONAL: A DETAILED LOOK INSIDE THE ACTIONS, WORDS, AND THOUGHTS OF KIP KINKEL

To look at a picture of Kip Kinkel, you would never have suspected that he was anything other than the typical high school student. With his brownish red hair and his sad brown eyes, he looked like someone who would knock on your door and ask if he could mow your lawn this summer or if your brother wanted to come out and ride bikes together. That this fifteen-year-old was actually a boy on the verge of committing multiple murders just wouldn't have seemed possible. However, that is just what he did. On May 21, 1998, he walked into Thurston High School in Springfield, Oregon, and shot and killed two students. He wounded twenty-three others, and at home, his parents also lay dead.

Of course, if anyone had had the chance to get a glimpse into his journal, they would have gotten the idea fast. Here now is a look at the life of Kip Kinkel from his birth to his sentencing, interspersed with his own words found either in his journals or the notes he left for people.

Kip Kinkel was born on August 30, 1982, to Bill and Faith Kinkel. He had one older sister, Kristin, who was born in 1976. Soon after he entered school, he began to have trouble. He had to repeat first

Kip Kinkel, the fifteen-year-old who killed two and injured twenty-three at Thurston High School in 1998

grade, and in second grade, he had problems with reading and spelling. He was tested for possible learning disabilities but was found to be in the ninetieth percentile on the intelligence test and so did not qualify for special education. In third grade he was still struggling and was retested. This time he did qualify for special education services. Fourth grade brought a diagnosis of a definite learning disability, but at the same time Kinkel was placed in a talented-and-gifted program because of his abilities in science and math.

> I sit here all alone. I am always alone. I don't know who I am. I want to be something I can never be. I try so hard every day. But in the end, I hate myself for what I've become.
>
> —*from Kip's journal*

Junior high brought increasing trouble for Kinkel. In seventh grade he and some friends ordered some "build-your-own-bomb" books from the Internet. He was caught, and his mother, Faith, was concerned about the influence of his newfound friends. In 1996 in eighth grade, Kinkel was caught shoplifting some CDs from a department store, and later that year, he purchased his first gun from a friend, a sawed-off shotgun. In 1997 Kinkel and a friend were charged with throwing rocks off a highway overpass. They were referred to the Department of Youth Services in Eugene, Oregon. A few weeks later the Kinkels took Kip in for counseling with psychologist Dr. Jeffrey Hicks.

Kinkel revealed that he felt unloved and rejected by his father most of the time and that he felt his dad always expected the worst from him. The doctor diagnosed Kinkel with major depressive disorder. Over the course of the next seven months, Kinkel had nine counseling sessions with Dr. Hicks. He continued to improve, according to the doctor's notes. During this period Kinkel was suspended from school twice: once for kicking another student in the head after being shoved and the second time for throwing a pencil at another boy.

> Every single person I know means nothing to me. I hate every person on this earth. I wish they could all go away. You all make me sick. I wish I was dead.
>
> —*from Kip's journal*

During Kinkel's sixth session the doctor recommended that he begin taking the medication Prozac, an antidepressant. It seemed to help him, but despite this, on June 27, 1997, Kinkel went with his father to purchase a 9-mm Glock. It wasn't to be his until he turned twenty-one years old, however. Kinkel's last session with Dr. Hicks was on July 30, 1997, and a few days later Kinkel bought another gun, this time a .22-caliber pistol, from a friend.

Kinkel began attending Thurston High School in the fall of 1997. He seemed to be doing well and stopped taking Prozac for three months. Soon after that, his father bought him a .22-caliber semiautomatic rifle, which he was to use only under adult supervision. The same day Kinkel made a speech in class on how to make a bomb and presented detailed drawings.

> The only reason I stay alive is because of hope.
> Even though I am repulsive and few people know
> who I am, I still feel that things might, maybe, just
> a little bit, get better.
>
> —*from Kip's journal*

October and December of 1997 brought the Pearl, Mississippi, and West Paducah, Kentucky, school shootings to televisions across the nation. Spring of 1998 added the Jonesboro, Arkansas, shootings. In May Kinkel bought a stolen .32-caliber pistol from a friend for $110. He paid for it at school and stuck it in a paper bag in his locker. When the gun was reported stolen, students were questioned. When Kinkel was questioned, he admitted to having the gun in his locker. He and the boy who stole the gun were both arrested and escorted to jail in handcuffs.

At the station Kinkel was fingerprinted, photographed, and charged with possession of a firearm in a public building and a felony, since the weapon had been stolen. He was released to his father just before noon.

> Please. Someone, help me. All I want is something
> small. Nothing big. I just want to be happy.
>
> —*from Kip's journal*

About 3:00 P.M. on the twentieth, Kinkel grabbed the .22 from his room, loaded it, and shot his father in the back of the head as he stood in the kitchen drinking a cup of coffee. He dragged the body into the bathroom and covered it up with a sheet. In the next few hours Kinkel fielded a number of calls for his father, telling everyone a different story about where he was. He also talked to two of his friends and said that he didn't feel well.

At approximately 6:30 P.M. Faith Kinkel arrived home. Kinkel met her in the garage, told her he loved her, and then shot her six times. He covered her up with a sheet also.

> I have just killed my parents! I don't know what is happening. I love my mom and dad so much. I just got two felonies on my record. My parents can't take that! It would destroy them. The embarrassment would be too much for them. They couldn't live with themselves. I'm so sorry. I am a horrible son. I wish I had been aborted. I destroy everything I touch. I can't eat. I can't sleep. I didn't deserve them. They were wonderful people. It's not their fault or the fault of any person, organization or television show. My head just doesn't work right. I want to be gone. But I have to kill people. I don't know why. I am so sorry! Why did God do this to me? I have never been happy. I wish I made my mother proud. I am nothing! I tried so hard to find

happiness. But you know me, I hate everything. I have no other choice. What have I become? I am so sorry.

—*Note found on Kinkel's coffee table*

What Kinkel did in between shooting his mother and leaving for school the next morning is not known. He left the house for school at 7:30 A.M., dressed in a long trench coat. He filled his backpack with ammunition and three guns. He taped a hunting knife to his leg and drove his mother's vehicle to school.

Kinkel entered the school at 7:55 A.M. Walking toward the cafeteria, he shot two students and then shot randomly into the cafeteria. By the time five classmates wrestled him to the ground, two students were dead and another twenty-three were injured. By 8:05, Kinkel was in handcuffs, and soon after, he was on his way to the police station. At the station Kinkel used a hunting knife to threaten a detective, and then he tried to cut his wrists. Police officers stopped him, and soon after, he confessed to killing his parents.

I know everyone thinks this way sometimes, but I am so full of rage that I feel I could snap at any moment. I think about it every day. Blowing the school up or just taking the easy way out and walking into a pep assembly with guns. In either case, people that are breathing will stop breathing.

That is how I will repay all you mother f——s for all you put me through.

—from Kip's journal

Police went to the Kinkel house at about 9:30 A.M. In addition to finding Faith and Bill, they also found bombs and other explosive devices throughout the house. By June 16, 1998, Kinkel was indicted on fifty-eight charges.

Before Kinkel's prison sentence was read to him, he stood up in court and read the following statement to the victims and their families:

I have spent days trying to figure out what I want to say. I have crumpled up dozens of pieces of paper and disregarded even more ideas. I have thought about what I could say that might make people feel just a little bit better. But I have come to the realization that it really doesn't matter what I say. Because there is nothing I can do to take away any of the pain and destruction I have caused. I absolutely loved my parents and had no reason to kill them. I had no reason to dislike, kill or try to kill anyone at Thurston. I am truly sorry that this has happened. I have gone back in my mind hundreds of times and changed one detail, one small event so this never would have happened. I wish I could. I take full responsibility for my actions. These events have pulled me down into a state of deterioration and self-loathing that I didn't know existed. I am very sorry for everything I have done and for what I have become.

On September 24, 1999, Kip Kinkel pled guilty to four counts of murder and twenty-six counts of attempted murder. On November 2, 1999, he was sentenced to 111 years in prison, without possibility of parole.

(Timeline and quotes from "Frontline" at www.pbs.org)

WHAT DO THE EXPERTS HAVE TO SAY?

Everyone has a right to their own opinions—and the experts in this chapter certainly have a diverse set of ideas—backed by years of research, interviews, and experience—about the causes of and remedies for school violence. They all agree on several aspects, however. They know that the problems and the solutions are not easy or simple, but are complex issues that require thought, effort, and a willingness to change from the culture and community as a whole to be effective.

Dr. Leo Sandy: Slowing Down and Service Learning

"We are living in a society that is 'adultifying' children," says Dr. Leo Sandy, associate professor of education at Plymouth State College in New Hampshire.

This culture is so accelerated—faster fast food, speedier cell phones, faster computers, quicker planes and trains—and in the process, people don't have the time to develop relationships. They are always moving faster and faster, but kids need time. They need old-fashioned stuff, like family activities and meals together, you know? Human contact! If we have no time for children's needs, they will become alienated and enraged. The world must slow down and spend more time on reflection and analysis.

Dr. Sandy has been fighting violence for decades and has been part of the antiwar movement since the 1960s. He writes articles for various magazines and conducts workshops. One of his latest pieces is called "The Nature of Peace" for *The Justice Journal*.

There are many factors involved in school violence. Today's acts are so over the top—such intense rage. Kids are becoming more and more disconnected with life. They sit inside and watch television and play video games where once they would have been out-side putting together a sandlot baseball game. Kids were not so pressured to achieve then; parents were less driven. Now kids don't have role models or real authority figures.

The solutions to the violence involve many different elements, according to Dr. Sandy.

We need the right programs. For example—not D.A.R.E. It's great for fostering good police/community relationships but it's like putting a Band-Aid® on cancer when it comes to taking drugs. We need smaller classrooms and we need teachers trained in the human element, not lesson plans. Parents must be partners in their children's educations. Children must connect with their school, their families, and their communities.

One of the best ways Dr. Sandy knows for making changes is through a process called service learning. This is a program in which students go out into the community and do something that connects with something they are learning in school. "For example," he explains, "students taking accounting classes can go out into the area's nursing homes and help people there with their taxes. It's a solid link between service and education. It's authentic learning—the best violence preventive I know," he adds. "It's not a quick fix but it is a great tool that holds tremendous potential for positive change."

In addition to service learning, Dr. Sandy stresses the importance of teaching cultural **diversity**. "School climates have to be accepting of multiculturalism—not as a slogan but as a reality; something we do, not just something we say."

Questions to Ponder

1. Do you feel that you are overly rushed? Do you have enough time for what you want to fit into your life? If not, can you think of something that can be eliminated, shared, or altered in some way?

2. What do you think of the concept of service learning? Is this something that would make academic material more meaningful to you? How do you think this method would change your way of thinking?

Service learning is a program in which students can offer others, such as seniors in their community, skills and knowledge they learned in school.

Dr. Fred Bemak: Community, Not Metal Detectors

Working with youth at risk for more than thirty years, Dr. Fred Bemak is an education professor at George Mason University in Virginia and the author of *Violent and Aggressive Youth: Intervention and Prevention Strategies for Changing Times.*

> My take on school violence is that we have had violence around for a long time, particularly in the lower income areas. However, now it has moved to the middle class and so it gets far more media coverage. If it happens in the suburbs it's a national event; if it happens in the inner city, it isn't. Location is what is making it more noticeable.

Dr. Bemak lists a number of reasons this violence occurs. "There isn't one factor here; it's a multitude of issues at multiple levels. It will not work to just try and simplify it with one to two simple solutions." Access to weapons in the home is one factor, but Dr. Bemak believes it goes way beyond that. "Kids get mixed messages from their parents and the media. They're told not to take anything from anyone. They watch movies with murders and killings that have no consequences or repercussions." In addition, Dr. Bemak looks at today's political climate. "I know it's an unpopular view right now," he admits, "but messages from the President like 'Get Osama bin Laden—dead or alive' aren't helping either."

What solutions does he suggest?

Putting in things like metal detectors just makes no sense. Control is not resolution and kids will still be violent. These kids are troubled. If that's the root cause, we can't address it with metal detectors. Walking through a detector won't make them any less angry. Instead, we must build a sense of family and commitment and to bring together the resources of mental, physical, educational, and psychological counseling to have a real impact.

Dr. Bemak sees a lot of potential in working as groups. "This is a very individualistic society," he explains, "and we need to work more toward becoming a collectivistic one. We need to work in groups to help foster tolerance and acceptance of others. We need to find ways to connect to each other in and out of school."

Working on the public-health level, Dr. Bemak trains counselors in school systems.

I tell them that you cannot give a one shot statement to kids like 'You SHOULD do this.' They just aren't going to respond. Instead, you have to suggest they try it, be willing to attempt it—to take a journey with you, work together and see what happens.

To combat this problem of school violence, we must combine awareness, knowledge, and skills together. We have to use our resources to create funding and find out what programs are working and which ones are not. In other words, we need to focus on prevention and start to build a community. Our society is overemphasizing control with aggressive youth instead of addressing the root of the problem. Planting metal detectors, dogs, and police in the schools' halls isn't working. We have to build a sense of ownership, pride, and responsibility into kids, starting by working with families. It's hard work, especially with disengaged and disenfranchised youth.

Questions to Ponder

1. Do you think the location of a violent incident changes how the media covers it and how people think about it?
2. Do you think President Bush's continuing "War on Terrorism" affects how you feel about violence?

Dr. Antonius Cillessen: Peers and Popularity

Born in Holland, Dr. Antonius "Toon" Cillessen has spent most of his lifetime researching middle childhood. An associate professor of psychology at the University of Connecticut, he has observed kids in grades four through ten so that he can better understand the dynamics of their relationships and the structure of peer rejection, cliques, and popularity.

Dr. Cillessen isn't sure that there are more incidents of violence than there used to be, but he believes that the violence has certainly become more severe. "The expression of it now is so much more serious," he explains. He believes that there are two main types of people who commit an act of violence in school: the reactive and the proactive. The reactive type is not well connected with his or her peers.

> These students are on the fringe and they are either very isolated or the targets of bullying. The loneliness or the pain of constant harassment makes them snap and do something violent. The other type is also some-what on the fringe but they have a sub-group of friends that usually have some pretty strange ideas. These are the guys who go on the Internet to find new ways to make bombs. Their actions are delusional, but they are very calculated and deliberate. What they both have in common, however, is that they are both on the outskirts of their peer system, not part of the mainstream. They are ignored or invisible.

In Dr. Cillessen's research he uses surveys to try to pinpoint just who is in trouble, and then he assesses that information to help the school develop a prevention and intervention program for violence. He encourages pro-grams that promote parent training, counseling sessions, and a focus on cultural diversity. "We need to educate kids that we all have different backgrounds and that one way is not better than another." "However," he adds, "even adults struggle with this issue." While he agrees that most of the students committing violent crimes in school are boys, he sees another trend developing. "Data from juvenile officials show that violence from girls is rising at a rapid rate," he says. "We really know very little about girls' aggression." He also says that violent kids may come out of lower economic backgrounds for several reasons. "The lower income families are less apt to turn off the television and just talk about things. They may have family problems without the money it takes to help resolve them and they just don't have any alleviation from daily stress."

> Adolescents are going through such a difficult time. It is a time of emotional and hormonal changes. They are all apt to do things impulsively, without real reflection on their actions. On top of this, violent television and movies plays a role by desensitizing kids and the access to weapons is certainly an important variable. For instance in Holland, only certain people are allowed to carry guns, unlike here.

Perhaps the solution to the issue of violence lies in research like Dr. Cillessen's. As he works to understand the structure of peer groups, friendships, and cliques, he might just grasp the answers to why some people just aren't accepted and who, in turn, cope with their feelings through vicious moments of power and ruin.

Questions to Ponder

1. Why do you think the incidence of violent acts committed by girls is increasing?
2. Do you think only certain people in society should be allowed to carry guns? If so, who and why?

Dr. Jana Martin: MTV and Sleepers

"I worry about the sleepers most," says Dr. Jana Martin, a licensed psychologist in private practice in Long Beach, California.

These are the kids who don't fit in, the ones nobody notices. They usually have low self-esteem, some slight learning disability and early academic failure. They aren't in any organized clubs or sports and they can't seem to communicate with others. They must look outside themselves for empowerment.

Dr. Martin knows today's kids. She used to run an adolescent inpatient program in teen group homes, and today she goes into schools to train teachers and to work with kids. She is both the president-elect of the California Psychological Association and the American Psychological Association's (APA) public education campaign coordinator for California. She played a key

MTV video jockey Ananda Lewis takes questions from teens following a screening of *Warning Signs*. Harold Branch III, one of the subjects in the video, and Dr. Jana Martin listen in.

role in the joint venture between the APA and MTV to produce an antiviolence video called *Warning Signs: Fight for Your Rights, Take a Stand Against Violence.* Consisting of three stories that show the pain and heartbreak that violence can cause, this video was shown on MTV for several months. Designed for use in middle schools and high schools, it went national in 1999. The timing was remarkable. "Our national kick off was three days after the incident at Columbine," explains Martin. "Here we had been planning it for over a year and they occurred at the same time." To date, the video has been shown to hundreds of thousands of students, and it is available free of charge to any licensed psychologist.

Dr. Martin sees many different causes and solutions to the issue of school violence.

> Suicides among teens are a sign of what is happening. There has been a 300 percent increase in the number of suicides among fifteen to nineteen year olds since the 1970s and it is the fourth leading cause of death for kids who are ten to fourteen. Our community leaders must be better trained on the warning signs to watch for in these children. . . . Violence is just a coping skill against helplessness. The media doesn't help since it gives the young killers so much attention—it makes them look famous and even more powerful. To say that this is just a phase is like saying just get through surgery without medication—you need help or you won't be able to do it. . . . Children have more accessibility to instruments of violence and that is coupled with the fact that they have more

unsupervised free time than kids had in the past. Their role models have shifted and are often aggressive and stability in life is usually declining.

Solutions? "We will never eliminate the problem, but there is so much we can do to control it," she says. "No one single approach will work. Each of us is wired differently and kids are individuals, but there is a hook for every single child out there, although it may be hard to find. Every kid does something well and it is our responsibility as adults in the community to find it and show how it can empower him/her." Dr. Martin's other suggestions are early identification of learning problems and appropriate treatment for them. "Kids who stay in school and feel competent aren't going to be violent," she says. "The problem with packaged anti-violence programs," she continues, "is that they are like old time revivals. People come into the school, get people all excited and involved and then they pack up and go away without following through with needed support. When they leave, so does the message."

"We simply must, as a community, help kids to communicate, not shut down. We need to encourage them to find any adult they can talk to—and never stop until they are heard," urges Dr. Martin. "We must teach them how to deal with today's stresses."

Questions to Ponder

1. How do you handle today's stresses? How do your friends? Which are the more effective ways and which can be destructive?

2. Do you think that the media's focus on violent youths makes violence more appealing to them?

Rabbi Yehudah Fine: Finding the Truth

Finding out what is important to youth is the primary mission in family therapist Rabbi Yehudah Fine's life. Author of *Times Square Rabbi: Finding the Hope in Lost Kids' Lives* and the forthcoming *The Real Dope: The Top 70 Questions Teenagers Want Answers to Today,* he has talked to thousands and thousands of teens to discover what they want and need in life. He was involved with the incident at Columbine in an ironic way. "I was flown into Denver to do a conference on family and school violence at the very moment that the shootings were happening," he says. "I spent the next several days on talk radio programs and being interviewed for newspapers."

"I have spent over a decade working with teens on the street and street gangs," says Fine, "but the main work I do now is the middle-of-the-bell-curve high school kids. I have surveyed over 14,000 students to date about their pressure points in life." Here is a portion of what kids have been telling him.

- More than 90 percent have a friend they think is suicidal.
- More than 95 percent have a friend who is seriously depressed.
- One hundred percent know someone who is using drugs.
- One hundred percent know someone who is using alcohol.

- Eighty percent can point out a neighborhood drug dealer.
- More than 85 percent have been pressured to use drugs and/or alcohol.
- One hundred percent have had violent language directed at them.
- One hundred percent are concerned about the violence.
- One hundred percent see and hear slurs, name calling, teasing, and so forth.
- Zero percent have declared not to use that same behavior.
- More than 95 percent are sexually active.
- More than 30 percent worry about someone they know going home to sexual, mental, or physical abuse.
- Eighty percent know someone in school they call a loser.
- Twenty-five percent know someone involved in a violent relationship.
- Eighty-five percent believe they will get a divorce if they do marry.

Fine's findings have led him to several different conclusions about today's youth. "Kids are in deep trouble," he says. "They have nowhere to turn, rarely any adult to connect with and they live in silence, unable to communicate with the older generation. Too many people are trying to tell kids what to do instead of listening to what they need and then empowering them by showing them what to do!"

Unlike many of his own professional peers, Rabbi Fine doesn't believe that violent games, movies, and music play a role in what is happening today.

There is just no correlation there. These kids are in trouble because they are neglected and no one cares; not a single study proves that violent media has any role in real life violence. In fact, some surveys show that kids who watch and play these things will actually calm down because it relieves their anxieties. To forbid them won't work. What should be done is to look and see is this kid being loved, listened to, asked questions?

What about gun control? Fine says empathetically,

We aren't going to get it. It would help, but it won't happen. Quick fixes are rarely successful. Instead, we must establish proactive programs that reach out into the community. They have to be based on the real needs of kids though, not what adults think are the issues. Kids have to feel free to share their secrets without getting punished. The bottom line is that we have to get to kids' questions and issues and then build programs around that. It takes a good counseling staff; schools need to put more money into counseling programs that take staff beyond the usual educational guidance counselor information.

Rabbi Fine also strongly believes that no one program will work at every single school. "Each school has different

Counseling is a key component that allows kids the opportunity to express their feelings and concerns about issues that are important to them.

kids with different issues," he says, "and professionals cannot just come in with their lectures, their information, and their solutions. It won't work. It must be based on the kids!"

As for family issues, Fine says,

> This isn't a 'blame game' on parents. They don't know how to connect with their kids and they keep either getting it wrong or sending mixed messages. Parents have to learn to talk—and listen—to their kids. They need to know that teens have messy rooms, they listen to weird music, they are attracted to disgusting people, they spend too much time on the computer, they get drunk and they get laid. However, that is all normal. It is when it goes from once or twice to chronic that there is a problem.

"It isn't rocket science to solve these problems," Fine concludes. "It just takes caring, respect, the freedom to ask questions, and an open environment. Kids are fortunately very idealistic—and this means they all still have the potential for hope."

Questions to Ponder

1. Do you agree with the rabbi's statistics? Do they surprise you?
2. Do you believe that violent videos, games, and shows make youth more or less violent? Why?

Phil Burns: Multiple Victims, Multiple Causes

The incident that first led Phil Burns to write his book *Multiple Victims, Multiple Causes* is one that he won't likely ever forget.

> I worked as a paramedic in the 1970s and one day, I got a call to a house where a father had beaten his wife to death. There was a young boy in the house and I had him ride with me in the ambulance. Now fast-forward eight years. I am still working as a volunteer EMT and I'm on another call to a home where a guy had beaten his girlfriend to death. You guessed it, of course. It was the same boy grown up and perpetuating the same cycle of violence. I saw it all first hand, and I came to believe that violence is toxic and it accumulates like toxins in the soil.

Burns is now the president and founder of a business in Oklahoma called SyTech Research. The company specializes in creating custom-made personality measurement tests, and in the process of putting the tests together, they researched the personality profiles of many violent people. "I wrote my book because I could see there was not just one remedy to violence—we're individuals and there is not just one cause. There certainly is never just one victim to any violent event either," he continues.

Burns puts a great deal of blame for the increasing incidence of school violence on poor parenting skills. Not spending enough—or any—time with kids can have some serious consequences.

> Parents are often in denial about how much time they spend with their kids. I tell them to 'suit up and get in the game' quick because by the time a kid is thirteen or so, the game is over. It's just totally over! The remedies for some of these younger kids is simple—involvement! Compassion! Kids need to know they have value. We lose more kids to suicide each year than to auto accidents; it's an epidemic and you know, parents have gotta give a damn!

The youngest suicide Burns has heard of was committed by a five year old. "Even at this young age, he was able to leave a note for his family that said, 'no luv' on it," tells Burns. "He just had no hope left—at five years old."

This attitude of caring and compassion shouldn't stop with the family, though.

As a society, we cannot ignore each other anymore. We can't demean anyone because we have no idea what might be going on inside their heads; we have no idea how much of an impact our words might have on them. I put it this way, 'Sticks and stones may break my bones . . . but words will hurt forever.' They can come back and haunt you. I encourage everyone to speak kindly to every single person they meet.

What about some of the other elements in today's culture that get a lot of blame for the violence?

Race is certainly an important factor. Some cultures glorify violence. The badder you are, the better. Die in a gang war and you will be glorified. As for gender, girls aren't dealing with testosterone levels and the pressure to be 'macho' but they also have more so-called accidental overdoses than boys do. Girls tend to take pills when they're miserable; boys grab firearms.

Gun control is not a big issue, according to Burns. "These kids would find some other tool to use," he points out. "It could be their cars, a knife, a baseball bat, or a rock. If the anger is internalized, it will explode. All that guns do is give the kid some distance between himself and the victims." Burns has interviewed a number of kids in prison who have committed some of the nation's most violent school crimes. "Every time," he says, "I find that their act was proportionate to the amount of anger they felt. Some of these kids still have no remorse and continue to be potential time bombs. It is frightening and very, very sad."

"It is little wonder that kids like gangs," concludes Burns. "Gangs give them purpose, caring, commitment, and discipline. In other words, they are family."

James Shaw, Ph.D., author of *Jack and Jill, Why They Kill: Saving Our Children, Saving Ourselves* also stresses the importance of positive parenting skills. In his book he tells about the 103 kids he interviewed in jail over a four-year period. All were guilty of what he terms "adolescentcide," or children killing children. Using a test he developed called the Homicidally at Risk Adolescents Profile (HARAP), he assessed all these kids. Every single test showed the same thing: all 103 kids had been deprived of unconditional and consistent parental love. They were also united by the fact that all of them felt unloved, rejected, and incredibly angry. These findings led Dr. Shaw to state, "It would not be an exaggeration to say that the weight and fate of the world rests upon the shoulders of parents." "Unsafe homes," he says quite clearly, "homes lacking in love, respect, and consideration, will equal, in time, unsafe schools."

Questions to Ponder

1. Do you believe that words can hurt forever? Have you heard words that have affected you negatively? Have you said words to someone else that were hurtful? What ways can you come up with to help lessen those hurts?
2. Does it all boil down to how parents treat their children? Is unconditional love the answer?

ALEX ORANGE AND STUDENTS AGAINST VIOLENCE EVERYWHERE (S.A.V.E.)

It was supposed to be fun; instead, it ended up being a tragedy. On a Friday night in 1989, Alex Orange, a West Charlotte High School student, went to a party to start off his weekend. When some people from the rival high school crashed the party, the trouble began. Orange invited them to stay, and he ended up getting shot and killed.

The following Monday, Orange's friend Angie Bynum, along with Gary Weart, a teacher at the North Carolina high school, had organized several hundred students to protest what had happened. Together, they began the very first chapter of Students Against Violence Everywhere (S.A.V.E.). From the beginning the organization stated that its mission was to "promote the virtues of peace, civility, and nonviolence by helping students of all ages learn how to respect themselves and other people."

Today, the program has spread nationwide. There are more than nine hundred chapters in the United States, with just shy of ninety thousand students taking part. Each month, another fourteen chapters and two thousand students join S.A.V.E. It is available at the elementary, middle, and high school levels, and it involves violence education and community involvement. In the younger grades, this information is part of the class curriculum. In the middle and upper grades, activities are extracurricular. Students are

Students Against Violence Everywhere

SAVE

Youth Voices, Grown-up Choices

National Association of Students Against Violence Everywhere
1-866-343-SAVE
www.nationalsave.org

S.A.V.E. is a national school-based organization that promotes student involvement in providing safe environments for learning.

asked to sign a pledge as part of the program and, more importantly, to make sure that they live by it.

Sample S.A.V.E. Pledge
I pledge to:
Work to make our school free from violence, drugs and weapons
Avoid violence at school and in my community
Work out problems peacefully
Help others work out problems peacefully.

S.A.V.E. Year of Peace Commitment
(Student Form)
I will not support violence against any person or any physical or verbal abuse based on race, creed or gender.
I agree not to bring a gun or any weapon to school or to any school event.
I will demonstrate respect for others and encourage those who provide positive role models for their peers.
I will tell my peers to seek adult assistance when conflict situations begin to get out of control.
I will support protection and consolation for victims of violence.
I will work to make our school and community free from violence, drugs and weapons.
I will oppose the use and glorification of violence in the media and our culture.

If I see a gun or other weapon on campus or at a school event, I will alert an adult about its existence.
I will be committed to nonviolent resolutions of conflict.
I will practice respect and love for the earth and all creatures.

By signing this commitment to peace, I pledge to support my peers in my community by examining my own actions and making every effort to practice nonviolence in my own life.

SIGNED _____GRADE _____

(This pledge also comes in forms for parents, teachers, and principals. Reprinted with permission.)

Robin Karr-Morse: Born to Be Bad?

When it comes to pinpointing the source of violence, the place it truly begins, one of the first people to ask is family therapist Robin Karr-Morse, co-author of *Ghosts from the Nursery: Tracing the Roots of Violence*. Now in its eleventh printing, Karr-Morse's book puts a completely different slant on why kids are growing up frustrated and angry.

> When kids stick a knife into a puppy as they lick an ice-cream cone, or when they stand in the middle of their classroom and shoot whomever they can, they

are simply reflecting what their brain once did or did not absorb. We aren't surprised when a child who has never had piano or violin classes cannot play the instrument yet we are shocked when a child who has never been shown empathy or nurturing turns around and attacks.

As former director of parent training for the State of Oregon and a member of the governor's Childcare Task Force, Karr-Morse has had a lot of professional opportunity to study children. She has also had personal opportunity, as she is mother of four, foster mother of two, stepmother of four, adoptive mother of one, and grandmother of one more. "I have been going to three cities a week for three years now doing presentations on my work," she says, "because violence brings the issue of childcare home to everyone."

Karr-Morse and her coauthor Meredith Wiley write in their book that the true roots of violence begin while a child is still in the womb and continue for the first two or three years of life. "The first year is the foundation of how we think and relate to each other for the rest of our lives," explains Karr-Morse. "The most important message I want to share with people, especially teens, is that what happens to little brains from conception on can drastically change what their lives will be like." Karr-Morse does this by explaining some basic knowledge about how brains grow and develop.

"A human brain develops from the inside out," she explains. "Unlike any other organ in the body, the brain is designed to need experience for the child to develop properly. While genetics may provide the blueprint, it is experience that executes that blueprint to its fullest potential." Karr-Morse's next lesson reminds one of being in anatomy and physiology class, but it has to be understood in order for her theory to make sense.

"The top layer of the brain is where rationality and reason can be found," she points out. "The brain cells from the center have to migrate or travel up to the surface to form this layer. They do this on strong, ropy fibers and as the billions of cells move, they meet up with others that guide them to where they are supposed to go. They give them the directions to their destination," she continues. "If they are sidetracked or they meet the wrong cells and go the wrong way thanks to the presence of alcohol, nicotine, or drugs, it can be horrible. It can result in many things from epilepsy to schizophrenia to ADD. Babies are rendered vulnerable before they are born," she says. Other elements that can negatively affect a baby's normal development are chronic maternal stress during the pregnancy and nutritional deficiencies in the mother.

The lesson continues. "Humans are the only species on the planet whose brains continue to grow at the same speed after they are born as they did in the womb. When they are first born, their brain only weighs twenty-five percent of what it will when full grown; by age two, however, it has reached ninety percent. These first years are a critical period for brain growth and we, as parents, either stimulate it with touching, talking, rocking, holding, and nurturing or we lose it. The window closes and cannot be reopened again." Karr-Morse likens this period of time to a child who has been born with cataracts. "If the cataracts are not removed during the first six months of life," she says, "the baby will be blind forever even if they are removed later. The critical period of the optic nerve development has passed and will not return." It is intimate and loving one-on-one interaction with a baby that will allow his or her brain to mature the way it was intended and to absorb vital subconscious lessons about worth, compassion, and love. Abuse and neglect will only impede the brain's development while causing it to grow and mature in unwanted, potentially dangerous ways.

If a new mother does not connect with her child, if there is no bond and the child is left alone, neglected, abused, or passed from one caregiver to another, the lessons taught will be ingrained for life. Not only has the child's brain been damaged during the pregnancy, but now child care is wreaking havoc. The child can easily come to believe that he or she is worthless and unimportant. The child will learn that his or her needs and wants go largely unanswered, and this creates feelings of anger and frustration, which can lead to violence. "All of us must first feel we are the center of the world," adds Karr-Morse. "Babies must bond with someone; if they do not, they will have an entirely different outlook on the world. How and who takes care of a baby is directly reflected in how many children we process through the justice system," she states unequivocally.

Karr-Morse and Wiley wrote their book because it stated what they felt the world had to know about child care. "We began a program called Healthy Start, which helped parents in the first three years," says Karr-Morse.

"It outlined a system of good prenatal care, parenting professionals making home visits to help new parents and answer their questions and provide training for them." Finding funding for this program has proved difficult, however.

> The message we want to get across is simple. If you have a child sitting in school who has been damaged in utero and has had a background of neglect, he can't listen to the teacher. He is in the fight or flight mode; he is looking around with constant vigilance, monitoring the environment for any sign of threat. He falls to the bottom of the class and gets labeled and medicated, becomes vulnerable to drugs and alcohol. He doesn't become part of the system; he commits a crime or a shooting and instead he and others like him feed the juvenile justice system. Girls run away, get pregnant too soon and perpetuate the whole assembly line. Where does it end?

Questions to Ponder

1. Do you think the first two or three years are vital to a child's brain development?
2. How would your answer to that change how you would parent your own children someday?

Elliot Aronson: Pump-Handle and Root/Cause Interventions

Ask Eliot Aronson the reason there is so much school violence today, and he will answer empathically that it has much to do with the school's non-curricular lessons on how people treat each other. In his book *Nobody Left to Hate: Teaching Compassion after Columbine*, he writes, "It is reasonably clear that a major root cause of the recent school shootings is a school atmosphere that ignores or implicitly condones the taunting, rejection, and verbal abuse to which a great many students are subjected."

In this book Aronson writes about how some solutions to the problem of school violence are superficial solutions he calls pump-handle interventions; they might help for a while and may even make a somewhat significant difference, but they aren't going to address the underlying cause like root-cause interventions will. Examples of the pump-handle interventions include better gun control, on which he writes, "Guns are not the root cause of the recent school shootings . . . but it would be naïve to suggest that their easy availability did not play a major role in these tragic events." On the issue of additional school security, he says, ". . . it should be noted that installing metal detectors would not make the schools perfectly safe. If teenagers with grievances and guns are motivated to shoot their fellow students, they can easily accomplish their mission without even entering the school building." He takes on the issue of violence in the media by commenting, "Millions of kids watch a lot of violent stuff on TV and don't go around shooting their classmates. At the same time, it would be naïve to believe that TV violence is not a contributing factor—especially if the youngsters watching all that TV are frustrated, angry, or prone to violence."

So what are the real solutions—the root-cause interventions, as Aronson calls them? One of the first goals should be to focus on teaching students emotional intelligence as well as academic intelligence. As defined by psychologist Daniel Goldman, emotional intelligence is a person's ability to be aware of, and to control, his or her own emotions. It involves the concepts of compassion, persistence, and, most importantly, self-restraint. "Our schools can and should play a vital role in helping students develop emotional mastery as well as academic mastery," writes Aronson.

Questions to Ponder

1. What do you think your emotional intelligence level is? Can you easily control your own emotions? Why or why not?
2. What classes could be offered in school that would focus on developing emotional intelligence?

AND NOW A WORD FROM PAUL HARVEY

One of this century's best-known commentators on society is Paul Harvey. Delivering news stories and comments on national radio since 1951, he has a reputation for making people listen and think. Some of his thoughts upset people, and this commentary is no exception. It brings up a lot of issues to think about, even if they are against what a person believes or thinks. Here is what he had to say in June of 1999 after the Columbine slaying.

For the life of me, I can't understand what could have gone wrong in Littleton, Colorado. If only the parents had kept their children away from the guns, we wouldn't have had such a tragedy. Yeah, it must have been the guns. It couldn't have been because of half of our children being raised in broken homes. It couldn't have been because our children get to spend an average of thirty seconds in meaningful conversation with their parents each day. After all, we give our children quality time. It couldn't have been because we treat our children as pets and our pets as children. It couldn't have been because we place our children in day care centers where they learn their socialization skills among their peers under the law of the jungle while employees who have no vested interest in the children look on and make sure that no blood is spilled. It couldn't have been because we allow our children to watch, on average, seven hours of television a day filled with the glorification of sex and violence that isn't fit for adult consumption. It couldn't have been because we allow our children to enter into virtual worlds in which, to win the game, one must kill as many opponents as possible in the most sadistic way possible. It couldn't have been because we have sterilized and contracepted our families down to sizes so small that the children we do have are so spoiled with material things that they come to equate the receiving of the material with love. It couldn't have been because our children, who historically have been seen as a blessing from God, are now being viewed as either a mistake created when contraception fails or inconveniences that parents try to raise in their spare time. It couldn't have been because our nation is the world leader in developing a culture of death in which twenty million to thirty million babies have been killed by abortion. It couldn't have been because we give two-year prison sentences to teenagers who kill their newborns. It couldn't have been because our school systems teach the children that they are nothing but glorified apes who have evolutionized out of some primordial soup of mud, by teaching evolution as fact and by handing out condoms as if they were candy. It couldn't have been because we teach our children that there are no laws of morality that transcend us, that everything is relative, and that actions don't have consequences. What the heck, the president gets away with it. Nah, it must have been the guns.

James Garbarino: Lost Boys

Psychologist James Garbarino has spent thirty years researching and writing about youth. His books include *Raising Children in a Socially Toxic Environment; Parents Under Siege: Why You Are the Solution, Not the Problem in Your Children's Life,* and *Lost Boys: Why Our Sons Turn Violent and How We Can Save Them.* He has interviewed and studied hundreds of troubled, aggressive teens, especially those who have murdered, and he is currently codirector of Cornell University's Family Life Development Center. He walks a fine line with his theory that while parents are responsible for how their children turn out, they are also not to blame. He believes that children are shaped by a combination of things inside and outside of the home. Unlike others, Garbarino feels that some kids are born with temperaments that make them likely to be violent and that even the best parents may not be able to save them from the effects of violent video games, poverty, gang violence, and other elements in what he terms a child's "tower of risk." He pinpoints a variety of factors that play a large role in youth violence, including depression, lack of a present father or mother, and violent movies. In fact, Garbarino feels that the link between violent television and aggression is stronger than the link between smoking and cancer. Each one of these factors is accumulative, with each new risk compounding the effect of the others.

The first item on Garbarino's list for improving the situation is gun control. He also suggests smaller schools, less television, and more involvement in community activities. One of his strongest tenets is the importance of spirituality in children's lives. He stresses that kids must recognize that life means something more than the physical living of it; that there is a larger meaning beyond their bodies. This helps to make them feel part of a bigger picture and to realize that life is sacred. He is a strong advocate of mentoring, or making sure that each child has a person in his or her life who cares and can help him or her deal with issues.

Dr. Perry's Core Strengths

Dr. Perry is an internationally recognized authority on children in trouble and brain development. He is the head of Child Trauma Academy, a center that provides research and training in the area of maltreatment of children and its long-term effects. He served as a consultant after the Columbine shootings as well as at other national crises, such as the Oklahoma City bombing. He looks at violence as a virus that exist everywhere and spreads quickly. He has created a program of six core strengths that he believes children need to protect them from society's violence. Called Keep the Cool in School, these steps include Attachment, Self-Regulation, Affiliation, Awareness, Tolerance, and Respect.

The first step in the program is Attachment, which refers to the ability to form and keep friendships with others. According to Dr. Perry, this is the cornerstone of all the other steps. Caring about someone, as well as trusting him or her, helps to give a student the foundation for security and healthy relationships.

The second step is called Self-Regulation, or think before you act. This step is all about recognizing one's emotions and then taking control of them. It puts a vital buffer between the thought or feeling (anger, frustration, fear, and so forth) and the action (violence). This is a skill that continues to mature as the student does and can prove to be a real key in how one responds to life.

Affiliation is the third step, and it's all about participating in activities. Perry writes that "affiliation is the glue for healthy human functioning. It allows us to form and maintain relationships with others to create something stronger, more adaptive, and more creative than the individual." Humans are social creatures, designed to work and play in groups. To be isolated and alone will create negative emotions. Affiliation helps people feel part of something, like they belong and are valued.

Thinking of others or just being Aware is the fourth step in Perry's program. It refers to the ability to notice other's feelings, needs, and values and is an integral part of communication and the ability to understand and learn from others. This ties directly into the next step, which is Tolerance—accepting the differences between people, whether it is sex, age, color, religion, or anything else. It goes beyond just noticing the differences and asks how one is going to react to them. If a student is open and flexible to these dissimilarities, he or she is more likely to see the worth and uniqueness of all human beings.

The last step in Perry's program is Respect for one's self and for others. If all of the other strengths are in place, this one should come naturally. As Perry writes, "When students respect—and even celebrate—diversity, they find the world to be a more interesting, complex, and safer place. Understanding replaces ignorance and respect replaces fear."

Questions to Ponder

1. As you read Dr. Perry's list of core strengths, can you recognize some that you need to work on? Which ones? What could you do to improve?

2. How do you react to other's differences? Do you catch yourself making instant judgments? What could you do to change that? Do you respect others and do you feel respected in return? If not, why?

Like these various experts in their fields, everyone has an opinion about where school violence comes from. However, the bottom line, which they all share, is that something is wrong with some of today's youth, and they want to keep talking, studying, asking, and researching until they find the solutions.

Questions to Ponder:

1. Do you think a person is born with a violent personality, or is it something that he or she learns? Why?
2. What can you do to make life feel more special or sacred?

WHAT ARE THE SOLUTIONS?

What can be done to make a real difference in the level of violence in schools today? What's the solution? Is it more metal detectors and security guards? Is it stricter gun control? Is it parenting classes for new moms and dads? The ideas are out there, and no single one is going to be the magical key that solves an incredibly complicated issue like this. Several ideas involve controversial issues.

Violence Prevention Programs

More than three-quarters of the nation's schools presently have some kind of formal violence prevention and reduction program in place, but how they are used and how effective they are is questionable. Most experts agree that the best programs are ones that address multiple issues, including both individual risk and environmental

Students talk and listen during an antidrug and antiviolence workshop.

conditions. They need to build skills and abilities, involve parent-effectiveness training, and make changes in peer involvement. They also need to have concentrated and rigorous evaluation and follow-up to see if they are really working. So far, they don't seem to be doing a very good job at all. According to a report from the Surgeon General, ". . . nearly half of the most thoroughly evaluated strategies for preventing violence had been shown to be ineffective, and a few were known to harm participants." Often this is not because the program itself is bad, but because it is not being properly **implemented**.

Effective programs must be multifaceted. They must create a positive school environment that builds and reinforces life skills and social competencies and help to teach coping skills and problem prevention skills. To do this, they must also have a simple, clear purpose or mission statement, a detailed way to teach these expectations, an unmistakable way to respond to anyone breaking the rules, and a way to monitor the progress of the program, as well as collect and evaluate the data from it.

Changing the School Environment

Three attitudes that could certainly help change the school environment, and thus indirectly decrease the risk of violence, are

- Care and Support: Schools need a nurturing staff, positive role models, support and mentoring from staff and peers, and an orderly yet accepting atmosphere. They need to have counselors who are trained in far more than educational guidance who listen, care, and know how to react when they see something serious or dangerous occur.
- High Expectations: Schools should expect good things from both students and staff. This means eliminating negative labels and focusing on students mastering at least the very basic academic skills.
- Opportunities for Participation: Schools should allow for more one-on-one time between staff and students; individual instruction is often very helpful. A culturally diverse curriculum is important in helping students learn to accept others, and parents and the community need to be deeply involved in the school, its students, and its curriculum.

Questions to Ponder

1. Which one of the attitudes above do you think is the most important? Why?
2. In what ways does your school provide a positive environment? Where is it most negative? What could be done to improve it?

Stereotyping

It is far too easy to fall into the trap of stereotyping students for the way they dress and act, and even for the words they say. For school staff—and even police and other authorities—stereotyping can create a certain profile that can supposedly identify violent youths. While profiling is completely understandable, it also creates concerns and is quite controversial. How much can authorities or anyone else depend on this stereotype? If a kid happens to be heard giggling with a friend that she was so embarrassed she could die, is she a candidate for suicide intervention? If a boy comes to school dressed all in black, should warning signs go out through the school that he is dangerous and needs to be monitored? What happens if he or she is ignored and goes on to pull out a gun?

Many mental health professionals worry that students will be further stigmatized if they are pointed out and mislabeled. The American Civil Liberties Union also worries that if this type of profiling becomes too rigid, students' rights of privacy, freedom of speech, and freedom to act and dress the way they choose will be trampled.

Another question that comes up with profiling is just how far it should reach. In a London newspaper in November of 2001, a new program was discussed that would profile any child thought to be at risk for committing a crime by the police or the schools; they would be added to a database for future monitoring. However, with this program, children as young as three years old would be watched for, as the article put it, "minor vandalism, nuisance, or an attitude of cheekiness." Not only would these children be watched, but it would be done silently and they wouldn't know—nor would their parents—that they were on this list. What behavior would qualify a child as potentially dangerous? Temper tantrums? Talking back? What would get a child put on the list and what could take him or her off it? The issue of just who would have access to this list is another factor to consider.

In "Early Warning, Timely Response," published by the U.S. Department of Education, the authors emphatically state the importance of not jumping on any student who has some of the most obvious trouble signals. "Early warning signs should not be used as rationale to exclude, isolate, or punish a child," they state. Teachers and other faculty must be very careful not to stereotype a child by gender, race, physical appearance, or socio-economic class when pinpointing who may be at risk. "It is important to avoid inappropriately labeling or stigmatizing an individual student because they appear to fit a specific profile or set of early warning indicators," they write in the report. "It's okay to be worried about a child but it is not okay to overreact and jump to conclusions."

Questions to Ponder

1. What do you think are the upsides and the downsides of profiling?
2. What stereotypes do you have about some of the people you have met? Are they valid?

Software Warnings

In the past several years some companies have created computer software to use in school systems that will help track incidents of school crime and identify danger areas. Three examples are the School Crime Operations Package or School COP, Mosaic 2000, and the School Safety Profiler. Each one works to keep track of information about the perpetrator, the victim(s), the weapons used, the location, and more in order to both help administrators watch for trouble in their own systems and head off problems before they start. These programs provide bar graphs, maps, pie charts, and reports so that schools can supposedly base their findings and changes on solid information rather than on guesses or hunches.

However, not too surprisingly, a number of people object to using computer software to analyze children. An editorial in the November 19, 1999, issue of the *Sacramento Bee* stated,

> There's something terribly wrong with the Mosaic-2000 mind-set: that if we can just find the right software program and feed it some surface characteristics of teens, it will assemble for us the three-dimensional understanding of them that so eludes us. Software is

no substitute for real conversations that need to take place, day to day, in American high schools. . . . Profiling is a fine technique for FBI manhunts; it is misplaced in American schools.

Norway's Example

Several years ago, three Norwegian high school students committed suicide because they couldn't stand being the victims of bullies anymore. This alarmed school officials, and so they had psychologist Dan Olweus, Ph.D., survey their ninety thousand students from all schools to see how many were being bullied and how many were depressed or distraught over it. The results were dire enough that school officials immediately decided to do something about it. Some schools reported as many as 17 percent of students were suffering from severe harassment. The Norwegian government created a three-tiered campaign in every single school to improve things.

The first tier consisted of community-wide discussions on ways to improve the bullying situation and befriend the lonely kids (thus involving parents, outside organizations, and so forth); special teacher training on how to recognize and deal with bullying behavior as well as on how to befriend the loner students; and videos about bullying shown to help students feel sympathy and/or empathy for the victims.

The second tier was made up of teachers presenting classroom lessons on how to prevent bullying and how to make friends with others; teachers organizing cooperative learning groups within their classrooms to talk about name-calling and other intimidating behavior and principals making sure that bathrooms, lunchrooms, and playgrounds were supervised consistently.

The third and final tier—if bullying still happened—involved school counselors who would conduct intensive therapy with the bully and his parents. Occasionally, a student would be moved to another class or school and efforts would be made to help strengthen his or her social and academic skills.

In twenty months bullying was down 50 percent. Olweus concluded that, "It is no longer possible to avoid taking action about bullying problems at school using a lack of awareness as an excuse—it all boils down to a matter of will and involvement on the part of adults."

Huntington Beach High School's Personal Approach

Huntington Beach High School was just an average American high school. With more than two thousand students, one-third were from various minorities. This school, however, took an unusual approach to curbing the amount of violence on its campus. Like most schools, it had already tried a stricter dress code and increased punishment for misconduct. However, inspired by Theodore Sizer, founder of the Coalition of Essential Schools, the school decided to try something different—the personal approach.

As writer Rebecca Martin Shore put it in her article for *Phi Delta Kappan* magazine, "Instead of asking the many to pay for the sins of the few, school officials launched a concerted effort to personalize the school experience for that small percentage of students who were engaging in disruptive behavior" (Grapes 2000, 115).

The vice principal of supervision, the school psychologist, the school nurse, and the community outreach liaison put together a list of students who didn't seem to be on the track to graduation due to behavioral problems. In addition, they asked teachers to list students they thought could use some extra help, and the district office was asked to list any students who had gotten three or more F's on their latest report cards.

All the lists were compared and cross-referenced, and then the program got started. It involved two basic steps. The first step was called the Adopt-a-Kid Program—adult volunteers were matched up with one or two students from the list. Their role was to listen, to supply any information that was needed, as well as to support and advise when asked. Some met frequently, before or after class, during lunch hour, or even sometimes during class, as class aides. Others met less often but always stayed in contact. This part of the program, powered by volunteers, cost the school nothing.

At the same time, the school staff met weekly to discuss the progress being made. "Most improved student" awards were created and handed out each quarter by the principal. Students also received key chains, certificates, and letters for their parents. The school created both a student-of-the-month and an athlete-of-the-month program. Twice a month the principal held a student forum in his office, during which any student was free to discuss a school policy, voice a complaint, or ask about upcoming activities. This helped students to feel their opinions truly mattered. Students began voluntarily wearing green ribbons once a week to show support for the school's new zero-tolerance attitude toward violence.

In addition to these steps, the principal of the high school gathered newspaper articles about local violence and put together a panel consisting of a juvenile court judge, a probation officer, a local detective, local police officers, and a mother whose son had been killed in a gang shooting. In settings of about 250 students at a time, students learned how the justice and penal systems dealt with violent acts.

The results of this different approach were quite remarkable. As Shore reports it, in the first year of the program,

- the school had the lowest expulsion rate (one student) and suspension rate in the entire district
- fifty-one percent of the students on the original list improved their GPAs
- seniors had the highest overall GPAs of the whole district; a first for the school
- test scores rose

In the second year of the program, the following changes were reported:

- forty-seven percent decrease in suspensions
- the list of struggling students was 51 percent shorter
- the Adopt-a-Kid program expanded to include peer assistant leaders

- Huntington Beach High was named the 1994 California Distinguished School

"No frills. No new funds. No grants," writes Shore. "Just some simple, low-cost efforts to personalize (Grapes 2000, 118).

Questions to Ponder

1. What are some of the negatives of a software profiling system, such as Mosaic 2000?
2. Why do you think things improved so much at Huntington Beach High School?

What About Homeschooling?

Homeschooling is growing at a rate of about 20 percent a year in the United States. While the reasons parents make this decision vary greatly from family to family, fearing for their children's safety is sometimes a consideration. Indeed, right after many of the school shootings of recent years, homeschool organizations were deluged with requests for information. An article in the April 6, 2001, issue of the *Houston Chronicle* by journalist Thomas Hargrove quoted Brian Ray, president of the National Home Education Research Institute in Salem, Oregon. "There definitely has been an increase in homeschooling because of the widely reported violence in public schools," said Ray. "Parents know that this is just a symptom of some very serious things going on in society. They have no good reason to put their children in harm's way." Current statistics show that there are from 750,000 to 1.7 million homeschooled students throughout the United States, and homeschooling is legal in every state. Certainly being at home reduces the risk of being injured by excessive school violence. Many parents also believe that the strong connections they have with their kids developed during the time spent together as a family will help their children be less apt to feel as left out, lonely, or different as they might have in the public-school setting. At home, labels like geek or nerd are rarely used. Parents also hope that the bonds they develop with their children will prevent any of them from ever becoming perpetrators of any kind of violence. While nothing can guarantee any person anywhere complete freedom from violence, homeschooling is one action that some families choose to lessen the risk. While many people thought the primary motivation behind homeschooling was religion, Ray said he

Homeschooling, a choice for about 1 million American families, provides a safe learning environment for kids.

found safety concerns were a priority even when he began a study of homeschooling eleven years ago. "Even then," he is quoted as saying, "parents told us that they were concerned about safety in the schools, whether it was fear of physical attack, or exposure to drugs, alcohol, pressure for premarital sex, or psychological pressure. The recent fatal school shootings have caused parents to believe that they are seeing just the top of the iceberg."

The Jigsaw School

Elliot Aronson and his graduate students developed a system called The Jigsaw School in the early 1970s. It is one that is still being used effectively by schools today. Aronson and his students were brought into a school in 1971 that had just been desegregated, and African American, Hispanic, and Caucasian students were together in the classroom for the first time. Within weeks there was a great deal of hostility and fighting, and so Aronson was invited to bring in his new teaching concept.

The Jigsaw School is one in which every single student is made an essential piece of a puzzle. Without any one of them, the picture isn't complete and the project won't work. It is a great way to learn classroom material as well as encourage listening and empathy. If the group does not work as a team, it will not succeed. The students depend on each other, which helps them to develop self-worth in addition to respect for others. Here is how it works.

1. The class is divided up into groups of five or six each, depending on the size of the class.
2. A theme or specific assignment is chosen for the class to study. This means the program can work in any subject classroom. If the system is being implemented in English class, for instance, the teacher might assign the students the topic of Charles Dickens, his story *A Christmas Carol,* and how it and his other writings reflected how he felt about mankind.
3. After the class has a topic, each student within the group is given a specific assignment within that topic. For instance, one person might have the job of finding out about Dickens's life. Another student might be in charge of reading and writing a

The Jigsaw School system promotes teamwork where each student in a group is responsible for a piece of a project.

report on Dickens's *A Christmas Carol,* and a third might investigate how popular Dickens was during his lifetime. A fourth might review the many films made of this story, and a fifth student might research the meaning of each character in the story.

4. Each person works independently to research his or her portion of the assignment. Later, he or she meets with the students from the other groups who are researching the same element, and they share information on their topic. This makes them "experts" on that part of the report.

5. Finally, the students get back together in their original group, and each member shares what he or she has found out about his or her specific assignment. If one person does not do his or her portion, that group will lack needed information and will not do as well on the follow-up test. This makes each individual essential to the group, just as each piece of a puzzle is essential to complete the picture.

After a few weeks of using the Jigsaw School pattern, teachers reported changes in their classrooms. Competition had been replaced with cooperation; feelings of acceptance and competency were higher and so were attendance and grade levels. This still proves true today, three decades after the program was created. A Jigsaw Classroom makes each person feel needed and appreciated, and that makes it a safer and happier classroom, too.

Peer Mediation Groups

This is a relatively new idea for improving the school environment, but one that is thought to carry great potential for making a difference. While there is not enough data at this point to determine its effectiveness, it does seem like a logical step in helping to diffuse a situation before it reaches the point of becoming violent.

The usual procedure in a peer **mediation** group is as follows: When there is a problem or conflict between two parties (usually two students), both of them agree to come in at a certain time on a certain day to meet with two mediators. Mediators are usually fellow students, but can include staff and faculty, too. The two arguing parties must follow a certain set of rules, including being respectful, listening to the other person, and waiting his or her turn to speak. Mediators will then listen, note some possible solutions to the problem, and then discuss the merits of each one until an agreement is reached. A contract is made, and both parties sign it. The mediators are then responsible for monitoring the parties to see if the promise is kept.

Increased School Security

One of the solutions suggested by various sources is increased security in the schools. Adding metal detectors, security guards, video cameras, spiked fences, and on-site policeofficers could certainly make an immediate difference, as opposed to other solutions, which might be effective somewhere down the road. Others suggest emergency alert systems, blast-proof doors and windows, motorized gates, and more frequent locker, backpack, and desk searches. However, at best, all of these address only one aspect of the overall solution. After all, a number of school shooters never entered the building; they shot from parking lots or across the street. Implementing any of these security measures is also quite costly.

There are many who are concerned about introducing more security measures into schools, too. They worry that it would make schools appear like prisons—and what might this mind-set do to the students? Elliot Aronson writes, "Installing metal detectors in all our schools would be tantamount to admitting that,

Security supervisors stand guard as students walk through metal detectors at Taft High School in Chicago.

from coast to coast, in small towns and large cities, in this, the most powerful democracy in the history of civilization, our teenagers are so dangerous and so out-of-control that we need to apply extreme measures to protect them from one another" (Aronson 2000, 56). How would this make students feel when they come to school every day? Are they going to feel more secure, or like inmates in a threatening environment? Can they learn in an atmosphere like that? Will it really make any difference? In the book *Waging Peace in Our Schools*, authors Linda Lantieri and Janet Patti write, "One fact is clear: the times have changed and we must face the changes. Kids are coming to school more frightened and more angry than ever before. And their fear and anger walk right through the metal detectors set up at school doorways."

Some changes have already taken place in schools around the nation. Ninety-six percent of schools now require that all visitors to the school sign in immediately. Eighty percent of schools close during lunch, so no one can come and go, and 53 percent have some kind of control over who has any access to the school grounds. Others are even giving out identification cards.

Questions to Ponder

1. Would you like to learn new material in a Jigsaw-type arrangement? What would you like about it and what wouldn't you like?
2. Do you think increasing the security in schools is a positive option? Which steps would be most effective?

A MESSAGE FROM THE RADIO

"Kids' Prayer" is a song written by singer Dan Bern following the Jonesboro, Arkansas, school shooting. His lyrics speak of the theories that abound about why this is happening and what can be done about it, and then propose his own concept of what needs to be done.

So sad, so sad, the news, come our way this
morning
Like a bad dream, a dream you never even talk about
In school, a school, where we send our precious children
The only place of innocence the world might ever let
them know
And barely aware of the odds against existence in the
first place
Of love and fertility of risk of a baby being born
And of clothes and food and fear and maybe relocation
Of sickness, recovery, of music lessons, painting the
garage
And lingering over eggs and thoughts and sleepy
conversation
And plans for the weekend, one last pause to pet the dog
And glance at the clock and the grabbing of the sandwich
and a notebook
Confident of nothing but the unbroken days that they've
been granted
But comes a child, a child so full of anger and hatred
Barely aware of the genesis coursing through his veins
With a gun, a gun, deaf and blind deliverer of madness
Skilled in its efficiency beyond his own unformulated brain

And with his hands in a fist, and his soul in a knot and
*   his heart racing*
And mind sick with images, his slim shoulders finally
*   feeling tall*
And his fellow creatures, students in their crushes and
*   their daydreams*
Struggling to unwrap the ancient secrets of geometry
And he pulls from his coat the instrument to shatter all
*   forevers*
In a random blaze of insides and blood and endless now
And boom and flash and again, and not even when it's
*   over*
Can any of them so much as summon up the sanity to
*   scream*
And on the floor his classmates blown down and choking
As he lays his weapon on his desk, partly sure he isn't
*   dreaming*

And all the world descends and offers up their condolence
And offers up their theories what went wrong and who
*   and why and when and how*
It's all the killing day and night on television
It's all the movies where violence is natural as breathing
It's guns and bullets as easily obtainable as candy
It's video games where you kill and begin to think it's real
It's people not having god in their lives anymore
Or it's all of it, or none of it, or some of it, in various
*   combinations*
Now all those theories sound pretty reasonable I guess
Though I ain't no scientist, I ain't no dissector of
*   statistics*
I ain't no theologist, I ain't no psychologist or biologist

142

All I can do is offer up a prayer of my own

Talk to your kids, play with your kids
Tell em your dreams, and your disappointments
Listen with your kids, and listen to your kids

Watch your kids, let your kids watch you
Tell your kids the truth, best as you can tell it
No use telling lies, your kids can always smell it
Cook for your kids, let your kids cook for you
Sing with your kids, teach your kids the blues
Learn their games, teach them yours
Touch your kids, find out what they know
Be sad with your kids, be stupid with your kids
Embarrass your kids, let them embarrass you
Be strong with your kids, be tough with your kids
Be firm with your kids, say no to your kids,
Say yes to your kids, take it easy on your kids
You were a kid not so long ago
There's things you know, your kids will never know
There's places they live where you will never go
So dance with your kids, paint with your kids
Walk with your kids, tell stories to your kids
One day your kids won't be kids
Maybe they'll have kids of their own
Let's hope they talk to their kids
Play with their kids
Tell 'em their dreams
And their disappointments

Uniforms

Although rarely a popular choice among students, some schools have adopted uniform codes as a possible deterrent to violence. What is the connection between them? Uniforms have benefits, including making students unable to wear gang colors, reducing the incidence of clothing

Uniforms promote a sense of equality, thus eliminating distraction and class distinction among students.

and shoe theft, eliminating the need for "clothes police" to make sure outfits are acceptable, causing fewer distractions, and creating fewer socioeconomic class distinctions. In addition, it instills discipline. Uniforms unite students by making them look more alike. They have less chance to ridicule others for what they are wearing, less chance of setting the rich off from the poor. Uniforms can be formal or casual, ranging from white shirts and ties for boys and skirts for girls to jeans and khakis with knit shirts for both. Students often object because they feel uniforms stifle their freedom of expression, and parents sometimes struggle with the cost of purchasing them.

In an elementary and middle school system in Long Beach, California, these same objections came up when the administrators made the decision to institute a uniform code in 1994. With more than eighty thousand students in the system, they made the program optional; currently everyone wears uniforms except for roughly five hundred students. Each school is allowed to choose its own fabric, styles, and colors, and grants are available to help families who cannot afford the clothing. Within a year the school reported that assault and battery in kindergarten through eighth grade were down 34 percent, physical fights were down 51 percent, and suspensions were down 32 percent.

The Role of Family

The evidence is in that families play a huge role in how children grow up and what pathways they choose in life. Changing the structure of the family, however, is one of the biggest challenges in this entire issue. The elements

A good relationship between child and parent is critical for parent awareness and knowledge of his or her child's feelings and thoughts.

of abuse (mental, psychological, physical), divorce, and inappropriate discipline are hard to change overnight, if at all. Perhaps the solution lies more in knowing that these elements are risky for kids and call for extra time and attention from parents and school faculty. Parents need to become more aware of their children's interests, their moods, what they are reading, who they are hanging out with, and how they are doing in school, beyond grades and attendance. Are they popular? Are they liked? Do they have friends? Are they showing any of the warning signs listed in the other chapters?

If parents suspect there is a problem, they must take action. The American Psychological Association reminds parents to do several things.

- Be available to your children: notice the times they are most likely to be talkative and be available;

start conversations; do one-on-one activities with each child; learn about their interests.

- Let your kids know that you really are listening: stop and listen when they talk; show that you are interested in what is being said; don't respond before it's your turn.
- Respond in a way children will hear: don't get angry or defensive or you will be tuned out; express your opinion without putting down theirs—it's okay to disagree; resist arguing points; focus on your children's feelings more than your own.

Questions to Ponder

1. How would you feel about wearing a school uniform? How would it change how you perceived other students?
2. Do you think a parent's involvement in his or her children's lives makes an impact? How so?

A Word from the Former President

In a speech by former President Clinton at T.C. Williams High School in Alexandria, Virginia, he stated, "There is really nothing more important than keeping our schools safe. And we've tried to do a lot of things in that regard over the last few years—having a zero tolerance for guns and drugs policy, putting new community police officers in schools where they're needed, trying to support more counselors in schools, more after-school programs, more mentoring programs, more conflict-resolution programs."

Zero-Tolerance Policies

In October of 1995, the Gun Free School Act was passed, which stated that each state that received federal funds for schools must expel for not less than one year any student who was determined to bring a firearm to school. Since then 94 percent of U.S. schools have adopted a zero-tolerance policy on guns; 91 percent have adopted a zero-tolerance policy on any other weapons, such as knives. However, to date there has been no data to support the effectiveness of suspending or expelling a student for bringing a weapon to school. In fact, in several cases it has only served to accelerate the student's anger and push him or her over the edge into action. Moreover, this has resulted in some schools taking the policy way too far, and some kids have been expelled for bringing a nail file or a pocketknife to school.

The biggest problem with zero-tolerance policies is that they are so rigid and absolute, so all-or-nothing, that they don't allow room for circumstances to be considered. For instance, students carrying rubber bands or slingshots on them can be expelled because these are considered weapons. A second-grader in Louisiana was expelled for bringing her grandfather's gold pocket watch to school with her because it had a tiny knife attached to it. Another student was expelled because her car had an ice scraper and pocketknife in it. An eighteen-year-old National Merit student was arrested in Florida recently. She was pulled out of class, handcuffed, and banned from her graduation. Her crime? She had spent the weekend cutting up some boxes and had left the kitchen knife in her car.

More complications to zero-tolerance policies ensue when a student happens to make a flip remark to friends and ends up getting hauled in to the police station and interrogated. This happened to a student who kiddingly asked his friend in shop class if he had a match while they were working with kerosene. Zero-tolerance policies are understandable; but they do as much harm—if not more—by not taking into consideration things like the student's background and school history, as well as the circumstances surrounding a situation.

Appropriate Aftermath Action

Another important aspect of school violence is how to respond while and after it happens. Weapons used in or near schools, suicides, bomb threats, hostage situations, and physical fights call for immediate action, and schools will need to have plans in place for what must be done in order to keep control of the chaos and hopefully lessen the trauma. Most schools will have—or should have—some kind of evacuation procedure that will help protect students and faculty from injury. Just as everyone should know where to go during a fire drill or a tornado warning, they should also know where to go in a crisis such as a school shooting. This will require an excellent communication system, with each person on the school staff knowing what his or her job is. It will also need to include a process for contacting the police and any other relevant support immediately.

Some schools practice these procedures the same way they do fire drills.

After the situation has been halted and the perpetrator captured, it will be time to deal with the aftermath of the crisis. Beyond just dealing with the physical injuries and/or deaths, there will be students who are emotionally or mentally traumatized by the entire incident. Two years after the Oregon shooting by Kip Kinkel, researchers sent out a fifty-page questionnaire to students who had been at the school at the time of the shooting, as well as to those who had graduated before the shooting, and a control group from another local high school. The following year, the results of the study were released. It found that the students who were closest to the areas of the shooting were four times more likely to startle easily at loud noises and three times more likely to be upset when they thought about the event. A quarter of the students at Kinkel's high school said they had been diagnosed with depression, anxiety, learning disorders, or posttraumatic stress disorder since the shooting (compared to 5 percent of the students who had graduated before the incident and 13 percent in the control group).

Schools may decide to have prepared crisis teams on hand to help students with their various reactions, which may include anything from suicide or paralyzing grief to insomnia or **paranoia**. Grief counseling is often provided for students and staff. This type of program often continues for weeks after the event as students try to come to grips with returning to school and picking up where they left off.

A Mixture of Possibilities

Here are just a few of the other things classroom teachers are trying to do to decrease the levels of violence in their schools.

- Beginning the school year with a list of class agreements for acceptable behavior and the consequences for misbehavior. Ideally, both teachers and students create this. The agreements are posted in the classroom.
- A Student Message Mailbox in the room, where students can post anonymous messages about things that are worrying them. The teacher pulls them out and reads them aloud for class discussion on a regular basis.
- Posters in the classroom reminding students of how they can control their emotions and feelings.
- Classroom brainstorm sessions on what alternatives to violence exist.
- Bringing in the antiviolence assembly program Rage Against Destruction to do a presentation for the school. This traveling organization started in St. Louis, Missouri, in 1997, and then went national in March of 2000. It is a free forty-five-minute program featuring a hip-hop concert, giveaways, and a short message "of antiviolence and acceptance of others in an interactive, entertaining and inspiring format." This isn't any garage band either; they have $3 million worth of state-of-the-art-video, lighting, and sound equipment. Each presentation involves a question-and-answer period as well.

Questions to Ponder

1. Which of the options listed above strikes you as the best one? Why?
2. Do you think zero tolerance is a good rule to have in schools? How could it benefit them? How could it be harmful?

**HONOR AND CHARACTER 101:
THE WEBB SCHOOLS**

Is there such a thing as a high school without any violence? Apparently so.

Situated in Claremont, California, about forty miles east of Los Angeles, are the Webb Schools. Covering seventy acres are two schools: the Webb School of California for boys, established in 1922, and the Vivian Webb School for girls, established in 1981. While the two high schools (grades nine through twelve) share the campus and meals, classes are all single gender. Each one has its own governing body, and between the two, there are about 360 students.

The majority of the students who attend come from California; others come from Alaska, Colorado, Washington, Oregon, Texas, Nevada, and Arizona. About 7 percent are international students from such diverse places as New Zealand, China, and Poland. Thirty percent are day students; they live close enough to go home at the end of the academic day. The remaining 70 percent live on the campus in dorm units.

One of the things that make the Webb Schools different from the typical boarding school, however, is their honor code. It is the foundation on which the schools were both built. "The primary mission here is character development," states Susan Nelson, who has been the head of schools for the past fourteen years. "We develop men and women of character here, where integrity and honesty are the foundation of their own identities." At the boy's school, the honor code stresses the basic core idea of right and wrong. The ideals of respect and fairness are enforced and expected—even if that decision isn't popular. At the girls' school, it is the same, with mutual respect and moral responsibility being the forces behind every decision and behavior.

There are no ethics classes at the Webb Schools— no antiviolence classes or Manners 101. Instead, that philosophy is built into every class and activity. Daily meetings reinforce the ideals and give the students chances to discuss things and figure out the best ways to behave. "We believe that this kind of education forms the underpinning for living that just doesn't leave any opening for violence," says Nelson. These daily meetings are used to go over anything from plans for upcoming events to coping with the nation's school shootings. "Talking about the shootings gave us all a healthy realization that no one is immune," says Nelson. "It was an opportunity to reflect on the enormous privilege we all have to be part of this school also."

While the school does have a chapel and the founder was a man of faith, the Webb Schools operate on a nondenominational basis, and there are no classes in religion, other than an overview of the world religions in history class. The school is geared to be a college preparatory, and according to Nelson, virtually 100 percent of the students do go on to college.

Uniforms are worn at the Webb Schools, but only on Sunday evenings and special occasions. The rest of time a very casual dress code is in effect, which Nelson terms "Southern California neat and tidy."

Other elements that make these schools unique are class size and teacher/faculty involvement. Most classes have about fifteen students, and the ratio of students to faculty is seven to one, far lower than the average high school. "There is very strong adult presence, guidance, friendship and time here," explains Nelson, "and that is what makes the difference. Because many of our students live here, our faculty is able to work or be with them on evenings and weekends. This gives the students close human attention and time to form solid relationships."

"We make a big deal out of any kind of verbal bullying, let alone anything physical," she continues. "We talk about intimidation and harassment. Our students also live together in dorms, so getting along is imperative."

Small class sizes, a good student-to-faculty ratio, and strong academics help to make the Webb Schools successful. What is the reason these schools are a place where violence of any kind just doesn't play a part? "We have a clear mission and set of principles that we follow," says Nelson, "and we are a small, nurturing community that truly loves and cares for each other."

WHAT CAN YOU DO?

The key to stopping the violence in school is, obviously, not a simple one. As there is more than a single cause, there is more than a single solution. While the government, the social service organizations, the psychologists, and the school systems each work to find answers and implement them, you and other students need to be aware that you are tools of change as well. It isn't enough to sit back and hope that these organizations and leaders will make all of the necessary changes, policies, and reports; you must realize that you have the power to make a difference.

You really do have a variety of ways you can work to change your school, your community, and even your world. They might range from signing a pledge such as the one later in this chapter to following the example of groups such as S.A.V.E. and starting a local branch. You also have the ability to govern your own behavior and attitudes toward yourself and others. You can read about and research the concept of teen violence and share what you learn with others. You can give speeches, hold fund-raisers, and write articles. As John F. Kennedy said a long time ago, "Ask not what your country can do for you—ask what you can do for your country."

Taking a Good Look in the Mirror

The best place to start any kind of change is with the person you see every day in the mirror. Boys and girls of all ages can make decisions that can alter their own lives as well as those of their classmates, and so can you.

For example, if you are experiencing feelings of rage, frustration, and loneliness, you absolutely must find someone who will listen to you and take you seriously. That is often difficult to do, but it is necessary. Someone out there can help you find the answers to your problems, or at least some temporary solutions until you are feeling stronger and better. In a videotape from the American Psychological Association called *Warning Signs: Fight for Your Rights; Take a Stand Against Violence*, a tearful Evan Ramsey is interviewed in prison. One piece of advice he has for other teens who are suffering from the same torment he did at school is this: "While you think you are all alone, you're not. There IS someone out there who cares— they do exist and they do care. Find them!"

If you or someone you know has feelings of rage, loneliness, or frustration, be sure to seek out help and find someone who will listen.

If another student confides information like this to you, you need to act on it; help him or her get help immediately. Talk of murder and suicide should never be considered a joke; too often it is an honest cry for help. Go to a counseling session with your friend, bring him or her to a peer mediation group meeting, or talk to your parents and see what they suggest.

If you see unfairness going on in school through bullying, teasing, or other unkindness, speak up! Few people realize how hurtful name-calling is, and if you can say something and put a stop to it, who knows what you might have helped to prevent. As Eldon Taylor wrote in an article called "Sticks and Stones Will Break My Bones, but Words Will Slice and Dice Me," "Words do more damage than things to most people . . . it's not the sanitary word itself that's damaging or fearful; it's the emotive value attached to the words." If you see verbal or physical abuse going on, do something. Tell a teacher; run to the principal; call your parents. Even if you aren't friends with the person it is happening to, you are a fellow human being with the chance to help someone in pain. Why not just reach out and do it? Be a role model for others.

Show others by example that you know how to settle problems without resorting to violence. Say no, walk away, laugh, get help, stamp the ground, run a few extra laps in gym—but don't use violence to find solutions to your problems, and help others not to do so either. If you see a big fight going on, don't stand there and cheer it on. Find someone who can help quickly and put a stop to it before the anger gets out of control.

Questions to Ponder

1. How can you change things for the better in your school on a daily basis?
2. What kind of role model are you to others? What could you do to improve?

THE STUDENT PLEDGE AGAINST GUN VIOLENCE

Started in 1996 by mother and veteran activist Mary Louis Grow, the Student Pledge Against Gun Violence is an antiviolence organization for all ages. Since 1996 more than 6 million pledges have been signed, and they plan to have millions more sign in 2003. To help accomplish this, the organization holds an annual Day of National Concern in October. At this event, which takes place in schools and communities across the nation, common activities include school assemblies and programs, radio call-in shows, the creation and wearing of buttons or t-shirts, public service announcements on local television stations, speeches by local officials, and, of course, multiple opportunities to voluntarily read and sign the pledge. Articles often appear

Seattle students march to call for an end of violence in the United States as part of "Day of National Concern About Young People and Gun Violence."

in newspapers, on the Internet, and in the news. In 2001 elementary school children in Georgia selected the theme "Hugs Instead of Guns" and attempted to create the world's biggest hug, hoping to get into the *Guinness Book of World Records*. A junior high in Washington State brought 650 students and staff out onto the football field and had a moment of silence as they came together to form a giant human heart.

The Student Pledge organization emphasizes that it is young people themselves who can often make a real difference in their world. The Day of National Concern is there to focus on, and remind them of, their opportunity. Their message is that "violence is neither inevitable nor an abstract force against which we are powerless. Violence is, rather, the sum total of individual decisions, and reversing the violence will occur individual decision by individual decision." The League of Women Voters of the United States says, "The Day of National Concern can focus discussion of the problem of young people and gun violence at both the national and community level, and will empower young people to see themselves as agents of change."

After students sign two copies of the pledge, it is suggested that they give one copy to a trusted adult who can remind them that they have a signed contract—a promise—and how important it is to keep that promise.

A number of different organizations and churches endorse the Student Pledge Against Violence, including the American Federation of Teachers, the National

Parent-Teacher Association, the National Education Association, Mothers Against Violence in America, the National Council of Churches, the American Medical Association, and the American School Counselors Association.

Below are two different copies of the student pledge; one for the elementary school level and one for the middle and high school levels.

Elementary School Level Pledge
If I see a gun, I won't touch it.
I will remember that any gun I see might be loaded.
I know how important it is to keep myself safe.

Middle and High School Level Pledge
I will never bring a gun to school.
I will never use a gun to settle a dispute.
I will use my influence with my friends to keep them
from using guns to settle disputes.
My individual choices and actions, when multiplied
by those of young people throughout the country
will make a difference.
Together, by honoring this pledge, we can reverse
the violence and grow up in safety.

Appreciate Diversity

Administrators often talk about cultural diversity, and what it boils down to is accepting others who are different from you. Judging a person's worth by what she wears, how he does his hair, what grades she gets, or how tall/short/thin/fat he is, is about as fair as judging people by their race, gender, or religion. So what if it is different from what you are used to? Isn't this a time in your life where you are striving to be different, to stand out in a crowd, to be liked and accepted for who you are, not for what shoes you wore that day or what kind of car you parked out in the parking lot?

Be empathetic. Have you ever felt out of place or alone in a new and unfamiliar situation? Can you remember a time when you wished anyone would just smile at you nicely or make an attempt to speak to you? Focus on those moments in your life, and then look around. How many others do you see who might be feeling the same way? What might a kind word do?

A good place to start is to become tolerant of others who are different from you and enjoy those things that make each of us individuals.

An old story has it that a young boy was walking home from school alone one day, and he dropped his books. Another boy helped him pick them up. Then, instead of walking away, as he normally would have, he stayed to talk, and within a few days the boys were friends. It wasn't until years later that the first boy revealed to his old friend that that very day he had planned to go home and kill himself because he was so lonely. Through the act of stopping to pick up some books, a life was saved.

Questions to Ponder

1. Could you have those same opportunities around you right now? What friends might you make and what lives might you affect deeply just by taking the time to be kind?
2. How much do you judge others before you actually know them? Do you think others do the same to you? How can that be changed?

Involve Your Whole School

Help the rest of your school to share this attitude. Talk to your school administrators about the importance of having peer mediation groups, anger management classes, and other helpful workshops. Set up a pledge event in your school; start your own chapter of S.A.V.E., join the letter-writing campaign of the National Campaign Against Youth Violence (NCAYV) (see page 175). Write skits, have assemblies, do role-playing in class, talk to your teacher about including some kind of antiviolence lessons in the curriculum. Have your English class write public service announcements and see if your local newspapers and radio stations will run them. Create posters and take them all over your community. Start making plans now to be a part of S.A.V.E.'s national Safe Schools Week. Held each year in the last half of October, this event offers the chance to address the issue of violence and draw the attention of the media and community. Some of the activities that S.A.V.E. suggests are

- challenge every student in your school to get to know at least one student that they currently do not know
- invite local law enforcement officers to make presentations to classes on everything from child safety to drug abuse prevention
- write a school safety public information sheet, flyer, or fact sheet to distribute to all the students
- put together a school safety workshop
- put up a suggestion box to solicit recommendations from students and staff on how to improve the school climate
- decorate a bulletin board at your school or in one of your local libraries
- coordinate a pledge signing
- put up a nonviolence banner on the front of the school
- hold contests, such as
  —*fight-free week*: give everyone some kind of reward if there are no fights for a week
  —*class level*: compete to see which grade level has the most signed pledges or the fewest fights

—*essay/poetry contest*: have everyone write on the topic of violence and then read the winning piece over the PA or at a special event

—*create a poster*: have everyone draw a poster with the theme of nonviolence and have students and staff vote for the winner, which is then displayed prominently in the school

S.A.V.E. also offers a National Safe Schools Week packet, which contains ideas, activities, posters, and bookmarks. Check out their Web site for ordering information for your school. There is power in numbers!

BREAKING THE CODE OF SILENCE: THE IMPORTANCE OF REPORTING

In James Shaw's book *Jack and Jill, Why They Kill*, he writes, "Kids who kill always tip their hand; their telltale behaviors have been visible and observed by *somebody* long before they picked up a gun and used it to kill people." Research has shown absolutely that every kid who has committed an act of violence has told someone first. They whispered it to a friend or boasted about it at lunchtime. They referred to it in front of a parent, confided it to a girlfriend, or E-mailed it to a classmate. This means that someone out there knew what might happen—and if this person had reported it, lives would have been saved. In a May 2002 federal study conducted by the U.S. Secret Service and the Department of Education, an

---

analysis of thirty-seven incidents of school violence showed that there were warning signs of the impending attack each time. "In almost every case in this study," says education secretary Roderick R. Paige, "attackers behaved in ways that caused others concern. Many had difficulty coping with a major relationship change or a loss of status among their peers. Many threatened or tried to commit suicide. And many felt desperate, and others knew that." In almost all of the cases, the person who knew was a friend, schoolmate, or sibling.

Some teens worry that what they heard was just a casual comment or a joke and they might be overreacting, so they stay silent. However, that is underreacting, and it can result in deaths. It's not a teen's responsibility to determine if what he or she heard or if the rumor he or she caught is true or not. It's an adult's job to determine the truth, but it is certainly the teen's job to report it. Every single uttered threat could be a serious one that could result in terrible tragedy. To not report something out of a sense of loyalty to a friend or classmate could easily result in someone's death or injury. It isn't a betrayal; it's helping a friend who is obviously suffering and perhaps saving many others from suffering at his or her hands.

Look at the examples that already exist.

- When Evan Ramsey came to his school on the day of his shooting spree, so many people knew what he was planning to do that one person even brought a camera.

- When Michael Carneal walked into his Kentucky high school with a gun, another student saw him and prayed he would make it through the day without hurting someone—and then told no one. Another had received E-mails from him giving him the details of the coming event. He said nothing.
- Clay Shrout called a friend and told him he had just killed his family and was on the way to school to take hostages. The friend said nothing and went to school, waiting for the shots.
- Scott Pennington's favorite topic of discussion with others was the different ways of committing a murder. He also told people how much he hated his English teacher and that he "was going to blow her head off."
- Barry Loukaitis told his friends how much fun it would be to go on a shooting spree and asked for help on how to reload a gun quickly. Before the shooting, he read a poem he had written in class that said,

> *I look at his body on the floor,*
> *Killing a bastard that deserves to die,*
> *Ain't nothing like it in the world,*
> *But he sure did bleed a lot.*

In almost every instance of school violence, other students knew the plans, helped get the weapons, saw the weapons, or heard the threats—and did nothing about it.

The good news is that, according to a 2002 report, more than 80 percent of teens surveyed stated that they are more willing to report a threat to school safety. They are speaking up and taking the information to someone they trust. That can be a parent, teacher, principal, relative, neighbor, counselor, or clergyperson. Anonymous calls to local police can be effective, too.

The list of potential disasters that were prevented by someone speaking up continues to grow. According to Ribbon of Promise, a group that organized to fight school violence after Kip Kinkel's school shooting in Oregon, eleven separate attacks between 1998 and 2001 were stopped because someone said something. All eleven were reported by students. Toward the end of 2001, a student reported a possible threat to the school, and authorities arrested three young teens soon after. Ages fifteen, sixteen, and seventeen, these boys had planned to blow up both Moffat County High School and the local courthouse in Craig, Colorado, as soon as winter break was over. They were held at a juvenile facility on charges of conspiracy to commit murder and to conduct terrorist training activities. Police Chief Walter Vanatta reported that these teens had the knowledge, skills, and capability to carry out their plot. "We have what are the normal problems of high-school age youth," he said. "As far as taking things to the extreme, this is a rare case."

Two incidents in early 2002 could have been added to the shootings list if it weren't for someone taking the time to report what was seen. On February 22 in Osceola, Florida, a ten-year-old boy came to school with his mother's 9-mm Glock handgun and pockets full of bullets. His mother discovered the gun missing and came back to school to get it without telling anyone. Fortunately, another student saw what was happening and reported it. The boy later stated he had brought it to shoot some of the kids who had been giving him a hard time. Just three days later, in Pinetops, North Carolina, a hit list of students and faculty was discovered and turned in. Minutes later, school administrators had two students detained for questioning.

When reporting an incident, adults will need to know everything they can, from the person's name and age to his or her reputation in school. Does this person have access to weapons? How do others treat him or her? Is he or she teased? Is he or she a bully? Does he or she use drugs and/or alcohol? Has he or she ever been seen with a weapon? Does he or she hurt animals, or has he or she committed other crimes? The answers to all these questions can help adults determine the seriousness of the threat and how best to react to it.

The U.S. Department of Education produced a report called "Early Warning, Timely Response," and in it the department outlined the following action steps for students:

There is much students can do to help create safe schools. Talk to your teachers, parents, and counselors to find out how you can get involved and do your part to make your school safe. Here are some ideas that students in other schools have tried.

- Listen to your friends if they share troubling feelings or thoughts. Encourage them to get help from a trusted adult—such as a school psychologist, counselor, social worker, clergyperson, or other professional. If you are very concerned, seek help for them. Share your concerns with your parents.
- Create, join, or support student organizations that combat violence, such as Students Against Destructive Decisions and Young Heroes Program.
- Work with local businesses and community groups to organize youth-oriented activities that help young people think of ways to prevent school and community violence. Share your ideas on how these community groups and businesses can support your efforts.
- Organize an assembly, and invite your school psychologist, school social worker, and counselor—in addition to student panelists—to share ideas about how to deal with violence, intimidation, and bullying.
- Get involved in planning, implementing, and evaluating your school's violence prevention and response plan.

- Participate in violence prevention programs, such as peer mediation and conflict resolution. Employ your new skills in other settings, such as the home, neighborhood, and community.
- Work with your teachers and administrators to create a safe process for reporting threats, intimidation, weapons possession, drug selling, gang activity, graffiti, and vandalism. Use the process.
- Ask for permission to invite a law enforcement officer to your school to conduct a safety audit and share safety tips, such as traveling in groups and avoiding areas known to be unsafe. Share your ideas with the officer.
- Help to develop and participate in activities that promote student understanding of differences and that respect the rights of all.
- Volunteer to be a mentor for younger students and/or provide tutoring to your peers.
- Know your school's code of conduct, and model responsible behavior. Avoid being part of a crowd when fights break out. Refrain from teasing, bullying, and intimidating peers.
- Be a role model—take personal responsibility by reacting to anger without physically or verbally harming others.
- Seek help from your parents or a trusted adult—such as a school psychologist, social worker, counselor, teacher—if you are experiencing intense feelings of anger, fear, anxiety, or depression.

Another group that is no longer active but did an excellent job in addressing the problem of school violence was the National Campaign Against Youth Violence (NCAYV). This organization ran a nationwide public awareness campaign that worked to reduce violence by and against youth. It had two goals: to increase awareness among kids ages twelve to eighteen—and adults—that violence prevention works and that there is a way for everyone to help a young person; and to increase resources for fifteen community-based prevention programs across the country to provide a standard for the rest of the nation. NCAYV had several suggestions for how students could play a part in stopping violence. Like the other antiviolence groups, it offered a pledge that students can sign. It reads

By signing this pledge, I make a promise to help stop the violence. I will work to bring peace by

- Talking with others about possible ways to make a difference where I live or work or worship or go to school
- Listening for signs of stress and frustration in my own voice and that of others without reacting in anger
- Learning about programs in my area for young people that give them the support, hope and skills they will need for success
- Taking action by writing to my newspaper or an elected official to encourage them to become part of the solution to youth violence

- Encouraging at least one other person I know to sign the Peace Pledge

The group also strongly recommended that students get in touch with the media to help spread the antiviolence message. They provided a sample letter students could use to initiate a community-wide letter-writing campaign (see page 175). The steps they suggest are the following:

- Choose your target (which media outlets—television stations, radio stations, etc.). Contact them to make sure you know whom to contact there. Confirm the person's name, spelling, and title.
- Research your community.
- Recruit help (neighbors, friends, church members, etc.). Get the street addresses or e-mail addresses and telephone numbers of those who would like to help.
- Involve youth.
- Pick a time to begin: a one- to two-week period is often best or the beginning of the school year often works well.
- Prepare a background sheet—this is a one-page description of the organization you want to promote—and tell how the group makes a difference in the lives of young people.
- Create your own sample letter (see below). Show your volunteers where, when, and to whom they should send their letters.
- Follow up with phone calls: make sure people received their letters and ask if they would like any additional information or an interview.

Sample NCAYV Campaign Letter

[Date]

[Letter writer's return address]

Dear [name of the news editor],

We never know when the next Columbine or Jonesboro will happen. And we don't know where it will happen. Unfortunately, if history is any lesson, we do know that the tragedy of youth violence will happen again, and somewhere an entire community of people will experience firsthand the anguish of losing their children to violence.

I am writing to you to enlist your help in turning the tide on this epidemic. Violence, we are told, is a learned behavior. How can the informational medium of [insert one: television, radio, newspapers] play a meaningful role in helping us to "unlearn" violence? In particular, what can [name of specific media outlet you are contacting in this letter] do to help our community reduce the risks of violence?

It is easy to point somewhere else when trying to identify the source of the problem. Some blame the media; others fault rap lyrics or parental neglect. The fact is there are many sides to this complex problem. But one thing is true: we can all be a part of the solution.

As the [news director, or other title of the person this letter is addressed to], you are in a powerful position to influence not only what news is covered, but also how it is covered. If youth see themselves reflected in the media only as victims and gangsters, then what choices do they see for themselves? If we want our youth to unlearn violence, we need more stories with images that illustrate the alternatives.

This is a request that you join our community's efforts to change the climate of violence. There are many ways for the media to make a difference. I ask you to consider only one: to bring us the news about how our community is rising to this challenge. Showcase the adult role models and youth who are part of the solution, and clearly identify how people of all ages and abilities can get involved in programs that give young people the skills and support that they need to succeed.

We don't want our city to be in the spotlight on other news programs across the country while people shake their heads and ask what went wrong in [name your city here]. Please help us to make a difference.

Sincerely,

[Signature of the letter's author]

An old song lyric states, "Let there be peace on earth and let it begin and end with me." Perhaps that sentiment applies here also; let there be peace in your school and let it begin with you. Do what you can, whenever you can, and start a new fad: one that wears tolerance, speaks understanding, and flaunts acceptance. Make your school hallways halls of hope, not of fear.

GLOSSARY

Attention deficit disorder (ADD): a syndrome characterized by difficulty in sustaining attention, impulse behavior, and excessive activity

Attention deficit hyperactivity disorder (ADHD): a syndrome characterized by difficulty sustaining attention, hyperactivity, and impulsive behavior

Desensitized: made less sensitive to something

Deterrent: something that prevents or discourages something from happening

Diversity: difference, uniqueness, or variety

Implemented: to put into effect

Irrevocable: something that cannot be changed

Mediation: action taken to help reach an agreement

Misnomer: a name inappropriately applied

Paranoia: mental disorder marked by a feeling of persecution

Psychosis: a severe mental disorder that often includes hallucinations

Qualms: fears or worries

Retaliation: revenge, getting back at someone

Schizophrenia: a psychotic disorder characterized by symptoms of thought disorder, delusions, and hallucinations

Stigmatizing: to treat someone or something unfairly by disapproving of them

Testosterone: a male hormone that causes a stage of growth in older boys

Unprecedented: never having happened or existed in the past

Vacillate: hesitate in choice of opinions

SELECTED
BIBLIOGRAPHY

Aronson, Elliot. *Nobody Left to Hate: Teaching Compassion After Columbine*. W.H. Freeman and Co., 2000.

Grapes, Bryan, ed. *School Violence*. Greenhaven Press, 2000.

Karr-Morse, Robin and Meredith Wiley. *Ghosts from the Nursery: Tracing the Roots of Violence*. Atlantic Monthly Press Books, 1997.

Shaw, James E. *Jack and Jill, Why They Kill: Saving Our Children, Saving Ourselves*. Gleska Enterprises, 2000.

FOR FURTHER READING

Fiction

Alger, Dale. *Dead Meat.* Superiorbooks.com, Inc., 2001.

Chessen, Sherri. *The Gorp's Gift.* Round Top Studio, 1996.

Koertge, Ronald, et al. *Brimstone Journals.* Candlewick Press, 2001.

Lorbiecki, Marybeth. *Just One Flick of a Finger.* Dial Books, 1996.

Myer, Walter Dean. *Scorpions.* Harper Trophy Books, 1990.

Strasser, Todd. *Give a Boy a Gun.* Simon and Schuster, 2000.

Zindel, Paul. *Beyond the Chocolate War.* Laureleaf, 1999 (reissued).

———. *The Chocolate War.* Laureleaf, 1991.

Nonfiction

Aronson, Elliot. *Nobody Left to Hate: Teaching Compassion after Columbine.* W.H. Freeman and Company, 2000.

Cruz, Barbara. *School Shootings and School Violence: A Hot Issue.* Enslow Publishers, 2002.

Day, Nancy. *Violence in Schools: Learning in Fear.* Enslow Publishers, 1996.

Grapes, Bryan, ed. *School Violence* (Contemporary Issues Companion). Greenhaven Press, 2000.

———. *Violence* (Teen Decisions). Greenhaven Press, 2000.

Hasday, Judy. *Columbine High School Shooting: Student Violence* (American Disasters). Enslow Publishers, 2002.

Jones, Jeffrey. *School Violence* (Teen Issues). Lucent Books, 2001.

Mazer, Harry, ed. *Twelve Shots: Outstanding Short Stories about Guns.* Bantam Doubleday, 1998.

Menhard, Francha. *School Violence: Deadly Lessons*. Enslow Publishers, 2000.

Miller, Maryann. *Coping with Weapons and Violence in School and on Your Streets*. Rosen Publishing Group, 1999.

Nuwer, Hank. *High School Hazing: When Rites Become Wrong* (Teen Issues). Franklin Watts, 2000.

Stewart, Gail. *Guns and Violence* (Understanding Issues). Kidhaven Press, 2001.

Web Sites

Center for the Prevention of School Violence
www.ncsu.edu/cpsv
This is a source that emphasizes how to keep schools safe and secure.

National Alliance for Safe Schools
www.safeschools.org
This organization provides training and research for school districts interested in reducing school-based violence.

American Psychological Association
http://helping.apa.org/warningsigns/
This site gives the list of warning signs of violence and other helpful information.

The Departments of Justice and Education
www.air-dc.org/cecp/guide/annotated.htm
This site features an in-depth report, "Early Warning, Timely Response: A Guide to Safe Schools."

Jigsaw School
www.jigsaw.org
This site provides information on how to implement the program in a school, along with resources, tips, and links.

National Parent-Teacher Association
www.pta.org/events/violprev/
This site provides information on preventing violence, including a kit.

National School Safety Center
www.nssc1.org
This site offers strategies and programs to help create and support safe schools.

Why Files
http://whyfiles.org/065school_violence/index.html
This site provides information on why kids kill, what can be done about the problems, and other issues for teens.

National Youth Violence Prevention Resource Center
www.safeyouth.org
This organization is a collaboration between the Centers for Disease Control and Prevention and other federal agencies.

US Safe Schools

www.ussafeschools.org

This Web site contains information, resources, and ideas for teachers and parents, including crisis management and safety plans.

The Webb Schools

www.webb.org

This Web site contains more information about the schools and their policies.

Student Pledge Against Gun Violence

www.pledge.org

This site offers information on recent events, the pledge forms, and more.

Students Against Violence Everywhere

www.nationalsave.org

This site features information on local and national events and different ways students can get involved.

Youth Crime Watch of America

www.ycwa.org

This is a youth-led movement to create a crime-free, drug-free, and violence-free environment in schools and neighborhoods.

The Surgeon General

www.surgeongeneral.gov/library/youthviolence/

This Web site features the in-depth report "Youth Violence: A Report by the Surgeon General."

The Child Trauma Academy
www.childtrauma.org
This is Dr. Bruce Perry's Web site which includes information on violence and other issues involving children and trauma.

Daryl Cagle's Pro Cartoonist Index
http://cagle.slate.msn.com/news/schoolshooting/
This Web site features some of the county's best editorial cartoons concerning school violence.

Organizations

American Civil Liberties Union (ACLU)
125 Broad St., 18th Floor
New York, NY 10004
212-549-2500

Center for Prevention of School Violence
20 Enterprise St., Suite 2
Raleigh, NC 27607-7375
800-299-6054

Center for Youth as Resources
1000 Connecticut Ave., NW
12th Floor
Washington D.C. 20036
202-261-4131

Connect for Kids
The Benton Foundation
950 18th St., NW
Washington, D.C. 20006
202-638-5770

National Alliance for Safe Schools
PO Box 290
Slanesville, WV 25445
888-510-6500

National Campaign Against Youth Violence Headquarters
2115 Wisconsin Ave., NW
6th Floor
Washington, D.C. 20007
202-687-1660

National Crime Prevention Council
1000 Connecticut Ave., NW
13th Floor
Washington, D.C. 20036
202-366-6272

National School Safety Center
141 Dusenberg Dr., Suite 11
Westlake Village, CA 91362
805-373-9977

Youth Crime Watch of America
9300 S. Dadeland Blvd., Suite 100
Miami, FL 33156
305-670-2409

INDEX

189